Josef Wallmannsberger (ed.)

T0247637

Executing a Renaissance

The Poetological Nation of Ukraine

UKRAINIAN VOICES

Collected by Andreas Umland

The book series "Ukrainian Voices" publishes English- and German-language monographs, edited volumes, document collections, and anthologies of articles authored and composed by Ukrainian politicians, intellectuals, activists, officials, researchers, and diplomats. The series' aim is to introduce Western and other audiences to Ukrainian explorations, deliberations and interpretations of historic and current, domestic, and international affairs. The purpose of these books is to make non-Ukrainian readers familiar with how some prominent Ukrainians approach, view and assess their country's development and position in the world. The series was founded, and the volumes are collected by Andreas Umland, Dr. phil. (FU Berlin), Ph. D. (Cambridge), Associate Professor of Politics at the Kyiv-Mohyla Academy and an Analyst in the Stockholm Centre for Eastern European Studies at the Swedish Institute of International Affairs.

Josef Wallmannsberger (ed.)

EXECUTING A RENAISSANCE

The Poetological Nation of Ukraine

Bibliographic information published by the Deutsche Nationalbibliothek

Die Deutsche Nationalbibliothek lists this publication in the Deutsche Nationalbibliografie; detailed bibliographic data are available on the Internet at http://dnb.d-nb.de.

Bibliografische Information der Deutschen Nationalbibliothek

Die Deutsche Nationalbibliothek verzeichnet diese Publikation in der Deutschen Nationalbibliografie; detaillierte bibliografische Daten sind im Internet über http://dnb.d-nb.de abrufbar.

ISBN (Print): 978-3-8382-1741-3

ISBN (E-Book [PDF]): 978-3-8382-7741-7

© *ibidem*-Verlag, Hannover • Stuttgart 2024

Printed in the United States of America

Contents

In memoriam

Олександр Іванович Кислюк
Classical scholar executed in Bucha, 5 March 2022

For

Polly Corrigan's Daughters

Rosie and Martha

Preface

Whoever may have hoped that the 'Executed Renaissance" of Ukraine, the annihilation of the most creative, innovative and productive poets, thinkers and artists in the 20ies and 30ies of the last century, may gloomily, but finally have receded to a distant past, a highly stimulating and controversial topic only for specialists in the fields of Ukrainian poetry, literature and philosophy, will have experienced a cruel reminder that history is not finished, not even past in an independent Ukraine fighting for its liberty and cultural survival against genocidal imperialist aggression.

'Executing Renaissance' as the title of this collection, responds both to the poets, thinkers and scholars again being persecuted and executed by the Russian soldateska, but also, in an attempt at existential optimism against all odds, made possible by the courage and determination of the Ukrainian people, insists on the monumental fact of the matter that Ukrainian intellectuals and artists are in the process of executing cultural and linguistic Renaissances in the most grim of circumstances.

This book has accumulated a remarkable list of debts I have come to owe to some of the most distinguished scholars in Ukrainian studies, namely Olga Bertelsen and Victoria Malko, whose intellectual generosity has proved to be without limits. It has been deeply moving to be able to include Polly Corrigan in this volume, a passionate scholar committed to Ukrainian culture, whose untimely death at 45 will remain with me always when meditating on Mykola Zerov's translation of Horace's Ode 2,3.

Professor Michael Goodman of King's College, London, Polly's PhD supervisor has been kind enough to revise her texts for publication, with my heartfelt thanks for his extraordinary kindness.

The editor of this volume has taken a vivid interest particularly in the Ukrainian Neoclassicists for a time longer than I care to remember, going back to 1984 conversations with Polish scholars in the basement cafeteria of East Germany's Humboldt University. Thus a dilettante's prolonged love affair, crucially depending on the generosity of the professionals like Olga, Victoria and Polly.

Joe Wallmannsberger

In the Sign of Zero(v)
Semiotic Walkabouts in the Imaginaries of Philological Futures

Joe Wallmannsberger

Die zukünftige Philologin, Zerstörerin des Philologen-Standes.
The future philologist, destroyer of professional philology.
(Friedrich Nietzsche)

Philologists do not usually aspire to astronomical precision in predicting the future, tracing the trajectories of stellar constellations with mathematical precision, that is, until they do. We are allowed to muster all our Copernican intellectual confidence and state with absolute certainty that from October 2024 we shall witness the global emergence of three interconnected planetary events, in the form of Viktor Petrov, Sofia Zerova and Mykola Zerov taking on their roles as fixed points in the planetarium of world literature.

The cascade of stellar genesis will be inaugurated by the German translation of the third part of Sofia Andrukhovych's novel 'Amadoka', in a truly lucky move to be published by Austrian Residenz Verlag (an echo most dim of the Ruthenian versions of Kakania's Reichsgesetzblatt.) The literally global presence will then be made an undisputed reality by HarperCollins having acquired the English language translation rights, most likely portending eventual major studio motion picture developments. Western audiences will come to appreciate the masterly and elegantly alembicated exoticism of Andrukhovych's narrative, turning the likes of Mykola Zero into heroes we had always already known, the complex psychological and historical networks of the epic stories we have educated ourselves to recognize, a vaguely and uncannily familiar template.

But why would characters from a country whose existence Western intellectuals had continuously struggled with placing on cultural and historical maps, not to put to fine a point on the basic geographical ones, have the potential to be turned into literary

household names in the boudoirs of Western literati? The great lev-
eller of war has proved to be the decisive force in also creating a
level playing field for the intellectual and artistic giants of the
Ukrainian tradition. The imperialist and genocidal outrage of Russian aggression has created cultural resonance spaces in Western
consciousness to detect the powerful and creative signals that had
been present all along for many decades, almost bizarrely ignored
by otherwise well-informed circles in the West.

And thus, it would seem that the literary and in a very precise
sense of the term philological future of Mykola Zerov is auspi-
ciously placed in the future. As one would have had to expect from
the author of 'Do dzherel!', this would be a case of serious delusional disorientation in the space-time warps of intellectual force
fields with dynamic horizons in the past.

In the Western imaginary, we will no doubt respond with surprise, delight and a movement formerly known as jouissance to the
recognition of new agents and actors in our digitally mediated theatres of consciousness: and let us not adopt too critically a reaction
to this happening, with Mykola Zerov being a figure to be reckoned
with in the cultural supplements of the leading papers a marvellous
addition to the canon. The presense and pretense of a figuration will
be magical, with the only caveat barely visible on the palimpsest:
this is not the real, which we have known all the while, not the unknown known ever present and pressing against the tectonic plates
of fragments of cultural repression and dissection. The real Mykola
Zerov, we will be deluding ourselves in experiencing in cinevision
in the not too distant future, represents but a reflection of a past
presens(c)e with infinitely more capacious energy spectra, an intellectual oscillation in the past generating its specific entanglements
with any potential future of the real. And thus we find ourselves
confronted not with a future Mykola Zerov resurrected from the
past, but a light afterglow of an unknown known force that had
been present in a schizophrenic dissection of Western consciousness over the past century.

Surely, you must be joking here, with Mykola being simulta-
neously present and absent, a moving target on canvasses of semiotic hallucination, not a real poet, thinker and philologist in 20th

century Ukraine, but a transfigurative perpetuum mobile, a shem tov for a world in need of redemption. If forced to take these ideas seriously at point blank range, one may opt for the figure of 'Zerov's Cat', a creature so scrupulously hidden in boxes, riddles and enigmas that being both dead and alive, present and absent at the very same time may appear to be at the very least a logically possible option. In the following walkabout in semiotic imaginaries and the often serendipitous experiments in detecting intellectual background radiation, we will consider options for philologists responding to futures in the ever present past.

The experimental set-up could not have been more basic and mundane, groups of students, international exchange scholars with any number of part-time Stasi activists added to the mixture, in the basement cafeteria of Humboldt University, East Berlin, sometime in February and March of 1984. (My notebooks still recall the subtle contretemps reliably created in using the very term East Berlin in conversations with GDR officialdom, with the mechanical correction of "Berlin, Capital of the German Democratic Republic" elicited in uncannily Pavlovian manner: the "unterschwellig feindlich-negative Einstellung" (inimical-negative attitude) remarked upon in the offical Stasi reports of my otherwise perfectly uneventful scholarly stay had been well deserved as it were.) An Austrian passport proved to be an efficient alchemical ingredient, as many Ukrainian poets and intellectuals in Galicia had experienced a long time ago with their Kakanian travel documents, in providing the bearer with an aura of undisputed impotence in terms of political power and influence, a court jester's identity card if ever there was one, so quite appropriate for the experimental probes into the unknown knowns of European poetic and literary undercurrents.

As if Kakanian aspirations of real world irrelevance and innocence had not been sufficient in and of themselves, one had added the persona of a student of the classics and of Ancient history, the perfect combination for an expendable personality in this precise context. The conversations with the East Germans proved to be determined by a Protestant obsession with the literal sense dominating everything, most impressively any kind of indirect, ironical or travestied modes of discourse. My bona fide interest in the parodies and travesties of the classics in the literary and intellectual histories of modern Europe provoked a most exhaustive and exhausting listing of classical echoes in East German literature, suffused with errands into the glorious tradition of 'Aneignung' ('appropriation', recently turned into a four letter word in cultural studies, one may want to reconsider in this context) of the salvageable remainders of bourgeois culture, such as Goethe, Schiller and Kleist among others. The penchant for literalness in my interlocutors very likely proved to be beneficial for all of us, not getting anyone in trouble in a cafeteria not offering 'melanges' out of principle. (In fact, I had developed quite a liking for the ersatz-coffee options, which in a comical twist of interpretations had then been taken to be a sure sign of "performative criticism" of the current economic conditions.)

The Polish students and scholars, conversely, showed a most welcome baroque receptivity to the modulations and transpositions coming into play in any parody or travesty of a classical subject, a taste for the hybrid that immediately stimulated a poetic and intellectual bond between us. Only three years after Solidarity in Gdansk opening up the horizon of being in the world and in the word in a fundamentally different mode, the Polish students gifted me with intellectual solidarity of the most decisive kind. During conversations over coffee black (real) and ersatz-coffee, my interest in Aloys Blumauer's Aeneid travesty and its enlightenment subtexts, had been understood, correctly and sensitively, as probing into the traditions of hybrids and counterpoints in the literatures and cultures of Eastern Europe, which in turn led to a canoply of most remarkable examples from Poland, the Czech lands, and, serendipitously, the literary tradition of Ukraine. Walking about in my personal dreamscape of ideas being gifted to me in unbelievably generous manner, and in many cases against all the odds, I should not be surprised if Jerzy Giedroyc himself had been present at our scholarly conversational encounters, Polish intellectuals opening up connections that had been present all along, but repressed by imperialist hallucinations of domination and homogeneity.

After detours via Adam Miskiewicz's poetic transfigurations of the figure of Spartacus in classical antiquity, a postgraduate scholar from the Jagiellonian University in Cracow, who had spent time as an exchange researcher at the universities in Lviv and Kyiv, remarked that a most extraordinary treasure was in store for me as an aficionado of classical parodies and travesties in Ukrainian literature, and then was kind enough to alert me to the name of Ivan Kotliarevsky. Hallucinating along walkabouts in European poetic imaginaries, we find ourselves transposed to the Maidan only a few years ago brimming with young people sporting tee-shirts with logos such as, 'Thank you Kotliarevsky' Or the first lines of his 'Eneida', „Aeneas was a brave and quick-witted bloke", and make no mistake about the real world importance of these images on the central junction in Kyiv, Ukrainian youth were shot for protesting consciousness of their cultural identity and desire for intellectual freedom.

The crucial problem the aspiring scholar from time-warped Kakania found themselves faced with was both straightforward and daunting, the regrettable lack of even basic linguistic knowledge of the Ukrainian language, very likely discarded and repressed in the innermost recesses of the kharmas of Austrian officers or teachers stationed in Galicia on the outermost fringes of the empires of the real and surreal. The fact of the matter was, it is all there, really, but to how to create methods of accessing the crevices in the European linguistic and cultural subconscious. A future philologist would be called for, opting for approaches beyond institutional accreditation and setting out to probe the real philological presences we have collectively taken pains to desensitize ourselves against.

Studying the 'Eneida' in farcical Champollion mode, first decyphering the hieroglyphs of the Little Russian language performing its debut in theatres of world literature, slowly progressing to the stoic philogical reader rhythms classical scholars have accustomed themselves to, finally reaching Epicurean bliss of being able to perambulate, slowly, haltingly and carefully, in the logographic gardens designed such elegant and sophisticated manner by Ivan Kotliarevsky. A private scholarly addiction, no value whatsoever to be attached in the transactions of the academic vanity fairs, or so it would have seemed for extended periods of time. The return of the poetic as the most real is anticipated in this minuscule philological epiphany, responding in anticipation to the world historical revolution of Ukraine's self-creation as a non-historical, but radically philological nation against all odds of imperialist genocide and logicide.

The initial exposition to Kotliarevsky's linguistic, exuberance and unlimited joy in hybrid modes, prepared the antichambre for engaging with forms of radical poetic liberation and philological transgression brought into play by the writers, thinkers and experimentalists remembered in the cataclysmic collection of the Executed Renaissance, an almost psychedelic excursion into what had been made possible and real in the collective poetic imaginary of Ukrainian literary pioneers in the 20ies and 30ies of the twentieth century. The book first published in 1957, and unfortunately still untranslated in its complete form, presents a literary and artistic theatre unfolding in Soviet Ukraine of mind-bending creativity, innovation and dialectical entanglements, conjunctions of the most archaic and the most modern (pace Walter Benjamin), the unfolding of the full spectrum of the potential and poetic vulcanism of Ukrainian language and culture. Literary scholars and intellectual historians—Olga and Victoria in this volume being leading figures in this ongoing conversation—have critically evaluated the merits and limitations of this, one would have to admit at least this, stroke of genius in finding an epithet for the intellectual reinvention of Ukraine in this period, and its tragically cut short developments. The one footnote we will no doubt have to add to this would seem to be that here again history is not distant, not even past, with Executing Renaissance being the abhorrent reality of Russian imperialist atrocities against Ukrainian poets, thinker and intellectuals being at the centre of the genocidal outrage, witness the merciless execution of Oleksandr Kysliuk in Bucha on 5 March 2022, a scholar of the Classics and Church Slavonic, whose only crimes must have been a love of the Greek aorist and the Ukrainian language. This is not history repeating itself, but rather the ongoing Executing Renaissance furor driving Russian imperialist hallucinations of a 'Russian world' purged of even the most innocuous traces of Ukrainian poetic and political autonomy.

A gentle, subtle and radical voice resonates with faint and distant echoes in the Executed Renaissance collection, with the finely drawn lines of a physiognomy reflecting in Proustian or Joycean mirrors, no trace of the wilder, even slightly dishevelled revolutionary portraits adopted by many of the creative, daring and dreaming poets and thinkers of the period. One could imagine perfectly well Mykola Zerov almost somnambulantly entering the class room in the Zlatopil 'gymnasium', which indeed he did almost every day of the week in what he later describes as one of the most poetically fruitful spells as a professor of Latin, Greek and Ukrainian literature before the war. The decidedly unheroic habitus assumed throughout his life stands in marked contrast to the radical project of inventing both a poetic universe of words and a poetic nation of free citizens out of the spirit of fundamental philology, a love of the word and the sign transcending any limitations of ideological regimentation, rhetorical fanfare or political machination. Mykola Zerov articulates the very idea and possibility of the future philologist, not formatted into the dominant models of semiotic production at any given time, but taking this absens(c)e as a motivating force to find real presences in a timeless continuum of poetic semiosis, the creation of the sign in the very process of being sublimated in a parrhesia of all previous and all future potentials of meaning and expression. Sounds like an attempt at high-octane contemporary literary theory, but Zerov as a future poet and philologist would be well placed to also take care of such rhetorical flashes and exuberance, assuming the stoic and laid-back interest in such constructions as befits the quintessential 'poeta doctus'.

The existential dimension of this radical philological persona becomes uncannily apparent in the table of contents of Maksym Rylsky's 'Vybrane', the 1966 selected poetical works, not allowed to be a full rehabilitation, with a ludicrously small print run, a preface determined in every word and sign by the poetic (il)licence the editor was forced to adopt if the chance of making Zerov's works at all in the Soviet Union: a classic and tragic sign of zero(v), the „Translations for Vergil's Aeneid" accurately list the passages Zerov managed to complete before his arrest by the NKVD, while at the same time pointing to the passages not available numbering and a line of dots indicating their absence. Standard editorial practice, one would have to assume in texts published in other countries at other times, but in 1966 Kyiv, readers would have developed the arcane arts of reading between the lines anyway, with the dotted lines referring to the sections of the Aeneid Zerov continued to work on and translate as an inmate of the Solovski political prisoner camp, during the night using scrap paper organised by fellow prisoners. These translations apparently were confiscated when Zerov was forced to board a transport to Sandarmokh in Karelia, where he was shot by NKVD officer Matyeyev in 1937. The material object of the lost translations will not be recovered, whereas Ukraine in its current fight against genocide and cultural annihilation is making its way through minefields to salvage the signs of the poems, the sign of Ukrainian language and culture as the inescapable conversational partner of the Greek and Latin classics of the best in European tradition.

It is precisely at this point in history, when Ukraine is fighting for its existential and cultural survival, that we can begin to explore the courage, creativity and determination of Zerov's philology of the future: same matrix again, war in Ukraine also in 1919-20, social and political upheaval, news of atrocities committed, dire economic circumstances, shortages of even basic supplies. A situation that would make Lenin ask, What is to be done?, while Zerov has the answer in, Under these circumstances, the highest priority must be given to publishing an anthology of Latin poetry in Ukrainian translations, in the most graphically and visually appealing form conceivable, and thus his 'Antologija', designed and illustrated by Hrihory Narbut, becomes available in 1920.

The 1920 book reverberates in the conversations had between Zerov and his friends in the Gulag prison camps of 1937, when the ode of Horace 3,3 proves to create a horizon for responding to the catastrophe they found themselves in, the poetic sage with a "professor" hat on his head, with an otherworldly view of a significant cosmos impermeable to the brutal realities of Solovki island. Meditating on his nocturnal translations and transfigurations of Vergil's Aeneid, evoking and empowering the beauty and creative potentials of the Ukrainian language, a projection of a future philology, the possibility of an agora, or Maidan, inviting free poets and speakers to find their voices that had been there waiting for them all along, voices no acts of delusional brutality and obsessive repression would succeed in suppressing in the future sign of the free word, sema or slovo (The C-shaped House of the Word may again have been shelled and bombed, but the shape of the freedom of the word they will not eradicate.)

The professional philologist of the present will no doubt detect doses of naive hero worshipping here, a nostalgic and romantic projection of wishful thinking unto a historical figure, clearly in need of deconstructive and critical debunking and reassessments. The crux of the matter with Mykola Zerov, however, we have to confront is his categorical rejection of any mode of self-proclaimed heroic existence or narrative: "If you are not born a hero, show no haste in trying to become one" he remarks almost casually to a friend in the Solovki prison camp, an elusive target thus for any attempts at recruiting the philologist of the future as an object of heroic transference. The scandal we will not manage to exorcise that easily lies exactly in the "professor" hat in among the barracks and barbed wire of the Gulag, capable of mustering the phantasmagoric powers of the liberating signs even in a situation of ultimate gloom. This must prove to be radically strange to our Western consumerist theatres of the mind, the "professor" hats being occupied with bigger salaries, bigger egos and the need for psychological counselling in view of the imminent dangers of academically induced burn-out.

We will have to take all the courage of breathtaking naivete, break the molds of professional philology — as destroyers of the 'Philologen-Zunft', an ironical mission f ever there was one — and fathom the real presences of the background radiation of the free word, always already present, turned into white noise by the machinery of academic content provision. The counterpuntal answer takes us back to Berlin again, in its schizophrenic modality yet another location, that is West Berlin in 1968: Alexandre Kojève stops en route from Beijing to Plettenberg, of all places, and radical student activists of the period enquire from the master interpreter of Hegel what would have to be their next steps in moving forward the revolution and liberation. The answer, even allowing for liberal use of psychedelic substances at the time, must have seemed somewhat unexpected, consisting in the succinct, "Learn Classical Greek!"

The (philo)logical consequence at this crucial moment in the global history of insurrection of free and significant voices against the regimes of repression and annihilation no doubt must be "Learn Ukrainian." The Ukrainian language as spoken and dreamt by future philologists of Mykola Zerov's calibre, a creative and poetic force resisting the powers that be against all odds, with Oriental submission to the fact that the logos of liberated signification will ultimately prevail. Against all odds, indeed, in that the economic and real world utility of Ukrainian in a global context may seen to approximate to zero(v), given the domination of digital media regimes pre-formating any conversation and prestabilizing the modes of expression available. The idea of composing a counterpoint to this totality of semiotic and intelletual regimentation in the form of adopting and adapting oneself to the Ukrainian language must necessarily appear to be sheer madness: yes, indeed, with extra doses of method added to the alchemical formula. Learning a foreign language is intended to make the unfamiliar familiar, domesticating the foreign, extending the zone of known knowns, thereby evading the decisive problem and challenge at the moment to make the world bubbles we inhabit stranger, alien and disorientating, as indeed they are in reality.

Liberating the future philogist from her entanglement with the still colonial and imperialist hegemonies of the mind, overt in the delusional rages of the Russian 'mir' and covertly repressed in German psychosis of history overcome, will entail the engagement with Ukrainian languages as the site and dramaturgy of this emancipation from self-created intellectual disenfranchisement. The rewards of this outrageously counterintuitive project are real and massive, in the first instance presented here being invited to the conversation between the Classical and Ukrainian modes of languages enjoying free love with and among themselves.

In the days when there was no independent Ukraine, but only a Soviet Republic, Jaroslav Rudnyckyj (1943) had to provide the key for Zerov (1920): The choice is much richer now, we will have to make the one worthy of the future philologist.

References

Andrukhovych, Sofia. Amadoka. Kyiv: VSL, 2020.

Nietzsche, Friedrich. 'Wir Philologen.' Colli and Montinari, eds. Gesamtausgabe. Berlin, 1980.

Rudnyckyj, Jaroslav. Lehrbuch der ukrainischen Sprache. Leipzig: Harrassowitz, 1943.

Wallmannsberger, Josef. Heteroglossaries. Innsbruck: IUP, 2023.

Zerov, Mykola. Antologija. Kyiv, 1920.

Zerov, Mykola. Do dzherel. Kyiv, 1926.

Zerov, Mykola. Vybrane. (Selected Works). M. Rylsky, ed. Kyiv, 1966.

Ethnocide in Soviet Ukraine
The Regimented Life of Mykola Zerov

Olga Bertelsen

The ethnocide in Soviet Ukraine, a systematic destruction of Ukrainian culture, religion, and identity by the Soviets, is better understood if placed in the context of Russia's colonization of Ukraine which took the lives of millions of ethnic Ukrainians over the last two centuries. The extermination of defenseless Ukrainian intellectuals and farmers en masse in the 1920s and 1930s, a calamity of mammoth proportions, remains abstract and conjectural unless scholars personalize the history of genocide and ethnocide in Ukraine, offering detailed histories of individuals who were identified as members of a "national minority" and political opponents by the Soviet authorities and thus were eliminated by them. Such personification of history conceptually combines two elements, a portrayal of people as enemies by the state and state violence aimed at erasing them together with their ideas, cultural traditions, and identities. This approach makes the state's genocidal intent and action more transparent and obvious.

Through an individual history of Mykola Zerov, a Ukrainian poet, scholar, literary critic, and translator who became a prominent intellectual in the twenties and thirties in Ukraine, this study attempts to expand the record of Soviet crimes in Ukraine that without the individual histories of people like Zerov have no name and have been consistently denied by the Soviet Union and, more recently, by the Russian Federation. Like many other Ukrainian intellectuals, Zerov was targeted by the regime for his Ukrainian consciousness, intellectualism, and unorthodox thinking, and was eventually killed by the Soviet authorities by an overly cruel and brutal method: he was placed naked in a mass grave dug by his fellow prisoners and was shot in the back of the head. Zerov's physical destruction was not unique or unusual in the context of the Soviet genocidal practices in Ukraine. However, Zerov's case exemplifies the Soviet ethnocidal and linguicidal practices — the intentional destruction of the Ukrainians' cultural identity, language, and national traditions, and ultimately a deliberate attempt to make the Ukrainian nation and its culture disappear.

Writing about Zerov, a victim of Soviet genocide, is as challenging as it is painful. It is challenging because Zerov had an extremely complex mind and left behind a rich intellectual legacy. It is painful because ferreting out something intimate and personal about Zerov reveals the enormous degree of suffering provoked by psychological and physical abuse imposed on him by the Soviet regime. The suffering of intellectuals whom we study makes us feel their pain, amplifying our affinity with them, be it the suffering inflicted by state violence in Zerov's case or domestic abuse as in Kafka's case.[1] Soviet society was not conducive to intellectual, creative, or artistic activity: the Soviet authorities strictly guarded the frontiers of individual freedom.[2] Under these conditions, it was extremely difficult for an artist to make a meaningful contribution to literature or art studies, and this caused great suffering for people like Zerov.

The physical survival of Zerov was more than questionable. He was doomed. The state had no need for innovative writers, independent thinkers, and melancholy figures. It needed loyal, passionately patriotic, and altruistic individuals, and crudely orthodox writers, completely devoted to the principles and ideals of the Soviet state. Zerov's incompatibility with the state was quite obvious, and it was a matter of time before Zerov appeared on the state's radar. In addition, the Soviet secret police worked tirelessly, identifying unorthodox intellectuals whose loyalty to the state was doubtful. The chekists systematically perlustrated their private cor-

---

1   Kafka's father verbally and physically abused his son.
2   Isaiah Berlin, *The Soviet Mind: Russian Culture under Communism*, ed. Henry Hardy (Washington, D.C.: Brookings Institution Press, 2004), 16.

respondence, and censored, confiscated, and destroyed their manuscripts.[3] Nothing was private, and no behavior guaranteed individual safety: the writers' self-censorship and silence, the defensive
mechanisms that many intellectuals developed, were equally sus-
picious to the state. They saved some lives, yet ruined a great many
others.

Zerov was a prolific scholar and writer, and his literary works
and correspondence with his colleagues and friends, his wife and
his lovers shed light on his sophisticated mind and literary taste,
offering a glimpse into the private space of fear and suffering inflicted on him by the politics and ideological climate in the 1920s.
These politics left no room for individual freedoms and creativity,
so much valued by Zerov. During this decade, state violence and
the secret police's brutality expanded in Ukraine quite rapidly, and
diverse literary discourses were curtailed and absorbed by the official discourse of proletarian art that served the party objectives. The
process of cultural modernization that was symptomatic of the
West during this time became impossible in the Soviet Union, and
Ukraine's intellectual elite faced nascent societal regimentation and
cultural isolation from the external world.[4]

As scholarship and archival documents declassified in independent Ukraine have demonstrated, repressions during the Soviet
era had a pronounced anti-national vector in Ukraine.[5] The Bolsheviks considered Ukrainians separatists and a potentially dangerous
force: from the moment they took power in Ukraine in 1919, the
Cheka/GPU/NKVD began to routinely collect data about the

---

3   Chekists are those individuals who worked for the Soviet secret police
    (emerged from the first acronym for the Soviet secret police, Cheka).
4   Solomiia Pavlychko, *Teoriia literatury*, 2nd ed. (Kyiv: Osnovy, 2009), 176–78.
5   Norman M. Naimark, *Stalin's Genocides* (Princeton and Oxford: Princeton
    University Press, 2010); Norman M. Naimark, *Fires of Hatred: Ethnic Cleansing in
    Twentieth-Century Europe* (Cambridge, Massachusetts: Harvard University
    Press, 2001); Yurii Shapoval, "Politicheskii terror v Ukraine—20–50-e gody XX
    veka: Tiazhkii gruz totalitarizma—poiski istiny prodolzhaiutsia," in *Ukraina
    Incognita*, ed. Larisa Ivshyna (Kiev: Ukrainskaia press-gruppa, 2004), 309; Serhii
    Bilokin, *Masovyi teror iak zasib derzhavnoho upravlinnia v SRSR* (Kyiv:
    NANU/Kyivske Naukove tovarystvo im. Petra Mohyly, 1999), 345; V. I.
    Marochko and Gèotz Hillig, *Represovani pedahohy Ukrainy: zhertvy politychnoho
    teroru (1929-1941)* (Kyiv: Vydavnytstvo "Naukovyi Svit," 2003), 52, 248.

moods and "nationalist" tendencies among the Ukrainian population in the countryside and in the cities, and especially among intellectuals.[6] In the early 1920s, through the secret police, Moscow took complete control over publishing production in Ukraine and established a sophisticated multifaceted system of censorship. In 1924, the GPU fabricated a group criminal case under the code name *Kyivskyi oblastnyi tsentr dii* (the "Kyiv Regional Center of Actions"), and Mykola Vasylenko, Ukrainian historian and president of the All-Ukrainian Academy of Sciences in 1921–22 (VUAN), was sentenced to 10 years in prison together with other scholars and teachers.[7]

To strengthen their grip on Ukraine, on 26 March 1925 the Central Committee of the RKP(b) (Russian Communist Party (Bolsheviks)) sent Lazar Kaganovich, Stalin's faithful adherent and follower, to Ukraine as the general secretary of the KP(b)U (the Communist Party of the Bolsheviks of Ukraine).[8] Under Kaganovich, the configuration of Soviet policies in Ukraine began to enforce Stalin's views, a factor that played a significant role in the lives of many prominent, and ordinary political and cultural figures in Ukraine. Ukrainian party leaders' attempts to criticize Kaganovich for his authoritarian management or, worse, their requests to replace Kaganovich as the general secretary in the republic addressed to Stalin, resulted in the methodical elimination of Ukrainian communists. By the late 1930s, here was no one left in the highest echelons of power who had been involved with the early implementation of Ukrainization, industrialization, and collectivization policies in the 1920s and 1930s. They had been accused of "nationalist deviations" and were eliminated by the state.[9]

The crusade against nationalist deviations in Ukraine that started in 1929 was characterized by a cascade of subsequent group criminal cases that obtained code names from groups allegedly

---

6   Cheka/GPU/NKVD are acronyms for the Soviet secret police.

7   Roman Pidkur, "V pamiat o 'politicheskoi tselesoobraznosti'," in *Ukraina Incognita*, ed. Larisa Ivshyna (Kiev: Ukrainskaia press-gruppa, 2004), 321.

8   Yurii Shapoval, *U ti trahichni roky: Stalinizm na Ukraini* (Kyiv: Politvydav Ukrainy, 1990), 46–50.

9   Ibid.

formed in Ukraine that struggled for political and cultural independence from Russia: SVU (*Spilka vyzvolennia Ukrainy* — The Union for the Liberation of Ukraine, 1929–1930), UNTs (*Ukrainskyi natsionalnyi tsentr* — The Ukrainian National Center, 1930–1931), UVO (*Ukrainska viiskova orhanizatsiia* — The Ukrainian Military Organization, 1932–1933), OUT (*Ob'iednannia ukrainskykh natsionalistiv* — The Union of Ukrainian Nationalists, 1935), and others.[10] The authorities broadcast the cases, publishing daily reports about the trials, cultivating popular belief in internal enemies and counter-revolutionaries. The show trials were preceded by years of meticulous work by the GPU that began its collection of *kompromat* (compromising materials) on hundreds of Ukrainian intellectuals in 1926.[11]

Moscow paid special attention to those who understood and resisted the central power and its intentions, and could articulate and convey their thoughts to others. The danger emanated from those who had an indisputable reputation as talented writers, scientists, and scholars. Those who established themselves as independent original thinkers, and who had knowledge of three or more languages were especially vulnerable.[12] Mass terror launched in 1929 by the SVU case that put thousands of intellectuals in prison was destroying "the social base" for Ukrainian separatism that might have put at risk the entire enterprise called the Soviet Union

---

10   Yurii Shapoval, *Ukraina 20–50-kh rokiv: storinky nenapysanoi istorii* (Kyiv: Naukova dumka, 1993); Olga Bertelsen and Myroslav Shkandrij, "The Secret Police and the Campaign against Galicians in Soviet Ukraine, 1929–34," *Nationalities Papers: The Journal of Nationalism and Ethnicity* 42, no. 1 (2014): 37–62; Myroslav Shkandrij and Olga Bertelsen, "The Soviet Regime's National Operations in Ukraine, 1929–1934," *Canadian Slavonic Papers* LV, nos. 3-4 (2013): 417–47; for more details about the SVU trial, see V. Prystaiko and Y. Shapoval, *"Spilka vyzvolennia Ukrainy:" Nevidomi dokumenty i fakty* (Kyiv: Intel, 1995).

11   Resistance of the Ukrainians to Bolshevik policies was manifested mostly in the Ukrainian countryside through individual efforts of peasants or groups of peasants. The Ukrainian intelligentsia in Soviet Ukraine had not been organized as an underground movement, a fact that determined their fate.

12   Dmytro Vedeneev and Serhii Shevchenko, *Ukrainski Solovky* (Kyiv: "EksOb," 2001), 64.

in economic and geo-political senses.[13] By 1933 the nationalist deviations among the Ukrainian party leadership were eliminated through party reprimands, public ostracism, and purges. The "nest of supporters of Ukrainian nationalists," the People's Commissariat of Education (Narkomos), was beheaded and purged. On 7 July 1933, the People's Commissar of Education Mykola Skrypnyk, who was harassed because of his supposed nationalism, committed suicide. Moscow ordered the massive purge of the entire Narkomos which lasted from 1933 to early 1934.[14] All of Skrypnyk's assistants were arrested. In total, 200 people were repressed from the Commissariat (in 1928 there were 202 associates in the office) for their national errors and deviations.[15] Between 1929 and 1935, as a result of collectivization and the Holodomor that eliminated millions of peasants, and the repression of intellectuals and clergy, the entire foundation of Ukrainian society was completely destroyed.[16] By 1935, Zerov realized that it was a matter of time before the GPU would appear at his doorstep.

It took the Bolsheviks a bit more than a decade to wipe out the pre-revolutionary "intellectual potential" of the nation that survived the revolution and wars. Sociologists, anthropologists, and historians typically characterize human losses on this scale as an event that eventually leads to a "cultural and spiritual collapse" of society.[17] A missing generation of scholars, artists, writers, and composers in one place foreshadows the interruption of national cultural traditions which in turn promotes pernicious behavioral

---

13   Marochko and Hillig, 149. In total, during and shortly after the SVU trial, 30 000 people were exiled for terms of 3 to 10 years, or executed as anti-Soviet national deviationists. See Prystaiko and Shapoval, 44.

14   Previous massive purges of the Narkomos occurred in 1929–30. See DAKhO, f. 15, op. 2, spr. 24, ark. 1, 2, 20, 31, 36, 51.

15   Marochko and Hillig, 7–10.

16   On the genocide in Ukraine committed by the Soviet regime during this time, see Victoria A. Malko, *The Ukrainian Intelligentsia and Genocide: The Struggle for History, Language, and Culture in the 1920s and 1930s* (New York: Lexington Books, 2021).

17   Marochko and Hillig, 286.

trends, characteristic of "post-genocidal" societies.[18] In a culturally groundless space and place, social connections and networks are problematic. Anti-intellectualism is celebrated and even considered a necessary attribute of survival. For Zerov, the repression of educators and intellectuals and their complete regimentation in Soviet Ukraine meant not only an intellectual vacuum and disruption of cultural traditions in Ukraine, but also a personal tragedy, associated with the impossibility to create, to live and, therefore, to be happy.

The Emergence of Zerov as a Scholar and Literary Wars in Ukraine

Zerov was born on 14 (26) April 1890 in the town of Zinkiv of Poltava oblast. He was fortunate to be born to a family where cultural traditions, history, and languages were respected, nurtured, and studied. His father, Kostiantyn Zerov, taught history and geography at the women's gymnasium in Zinkiv, and inspired his son's love for classical languages and literatures. Maria Yaresko, Zerov's mother, was of free Cossack origin. Although her husband gravitated toward the Russian culture, she raised her children to love and respect the Ukrainian language and culture which established the foundations of Zerov's national consciousness. Growing up fully bilingual, he highly appreciated and romanticized the Yaresko family's roots of the Left Bank Cossack aristocracy.[19]

While Zerov was a student at the First Kyiv gymnasium, his Ukrainian identity was reinforced by the influence of two individuals—Stanislav Trubsh who taught classical languages there, including Latin, and Mykola Liatoshynskyi, a teacher of history and a librarian at the gymnasium. Interestingly enough, among Trubsh's students were also Maksym Rylskyi and Oswald

---

18   See James Mace's works on the "post-genocidal" Ukrainian society, for instance, his *Vashi mertvi vybraly mene...*, ed. Larysa Ivshyna (Kyiv: Vydavnytstvo ZAT "Ukrains'ka pres-grupa," 2008), 457–58.

19   Volodymyr Panchenko, "Molodi lita Mykoly Zerova," in *Kiltsia na derevi* by Volodymyr Panchenko (Kyiv: Klio, 2015), 56–59; Ivan Dziuba, "Z kastalskykh dzherel krasy. Mykola Zerov," in *Mykola Zerov: Vybrani tvory*, ed. Volodymyr Panchenko (Kyiv: Smoloskyp, 2015), 9 (9–63).

Burghardt, future poets who, like Zerov, were also eternally grateful to Trubsh for forming their aesthetic views and appreciation of history and antiquity, including its culture and art. All three students became known as "neoclassicists" in the twenties.[20]

Zerov was very well-organized and self-disciplined.[21] At an early stage as a university student, in 1911–1912, he began to publish his literary essays and book reviews in the journal *The Light* (Svitlo). Zerov also became the author of mature literary critical articles that he published in the newspaper *Council* (Rada). By 1913, his philosophical views were refined and sophisticated: he distanced himself from populist ideas, envisioning future Ukrainian literature as the product of modernization, artistic beauty, and eclectic diversity.[22] Very quickly, Zerov established a reputation as an erudite, but, beyond that, those who knew Zerov closely mentioned his rare faculty, a photographic memory which might have helped him become a talented poet and brilliant translator.[23] His thirst for a Ukrainian printed word, especially *starodruky* ("ancient" prints), further shaped his Ukrainian consciousness and lexicon. A library (any library!) was magic for Zerov. A true bibliophile, he spent a great deal of time in libraries.[24] His culturalism, however, did not obscure his understanding of the politics of the Ukrainian question. He was painfully aware of the colonial status of Ukrainian culture, the process of assimilation and russification among the Ukrainian youth, and the problem of banality and cultural provincialism among the Ukrainian literati, addressing these issues in his critical essays.

Zerov's intellectual and national space was expanded during his student years at the Kyiv University's Philological School, when he began to attend the Ukrainian club "Family" (Rodyna), led by Mykola Lysenko, that opened in 1908 on Volodymyrska Street in Kyiv. Zerov discovered the Ukrainian Kyiv that absorbed the traditions of intellectualism and Ukrainianness inherent in the Lysenko,

---

20   Panchenko, *Kiltsia na derevi*, 62–63.
21   Panchenko, *Kiltsia na derevi*, 105.
22   Panchenko, *Kiltsia na derevi*, 92.
23   Panchenko, *Kiltsia na derevi*, 63, 105.
24   Panchenko, *Kiltsia na derevi*, 73–74, 84, 89.

the Kosach, and the Starytskyi families.[25] By 1914, when Zerov began teaching at a gymnasium in Zlatopil, a prosperous Jewish shtetl in central Ukraine, he earned the reputation of a polyglot and an intellectual, and a wonderful teacher and public speaker. Interestingly, the Ukrainian distinguished historian and a prominent political figure Mykhailo Hrushevsky's cousin Hryhorii Hrushevsky also taught at the Zlatopil gymnasium. There is some evidence to suggest that Hrushevsky contributed greatly to the formation of Zerov's Ukrainian consciousness, as they collaborated on a number of projects, and even discussed the prospect of transforming the gymnasium into an institute of higher education.[26] It was distressing for Zerov to observe how the imperial authorities annihilated the Ukrainian language at the beginning of the First World War, closing "Prosvita" and the Ukrainian journals.[27]

The years Zerov spent in Zlatopil were extremely productive. He translated the ancient Roman poets Vergil, Horace, and Catullus, but was able to publish his translations only in 1920 in Kyiv as an anthology of Roman poetry.[28] Inspired by the ideas of Ukrainian national liberation, Zerov returned to Kyiv in 1917, a move that was also provoked by his inner crisis and nervous break: he was professionally ambitious, and he believed the new revolutionary Kyiv was the place where he could realize himself as a scholar, teacher, and writer.

In 1917, Zerov began to teach Latin at the newly established Second Ukrainian State gymnasium named after the Brotherhood of Saints Cyril and Methodius. In the evenings, from 1918 to 1920, he also taught Ukrainian language and culture at the Kyiv Architectural Institute. There were certainly pragmatic considerations for

---

25 Panchenko, *Kiltsia na derevi*, 75.
26 Panchenko, *Kiltsia na derevi*, 115–16.
27 Prosvita, a network of Ukrainian community educational organizations, functioned in Ukraine from the late 1860s to the 1940s, and in other countries from the beginning of twentieth century. Prosvita was instrumental for shaping the Ukrainians' national identity and the Ukrainian national movement. See Bohdan Kravtsiv, Mykhailo Borovsky, Vasyl Markus, and Avhustyn Shtefan, "Prosvita Societies," *Encyclopedia of Ukraine*, ed. Danylo Husar Struk, vol. 4 (Toronto, CA: University of Toronto Press Incorporated, 1993), 245–252.
28 Panchenko, *Kiltsia na derevi*, 117.

taking extra hours, as it was financially difficult for teachers and professors in Ukraine to get through these turbulent years. Yet there was another reason for Zerov's extreme overload and hectic schedule: there were simply not enough Ukrainian specialists who could teach at gymnasiums and universities at the time.[29]

Courtesy of TsDAMLIMU (the Central State Archive-Museum of Literature and Art in Ukraine), fond 28, op. 1, spr. 218, ark. 6.
Mykola Zerov and Sofiia Zerova. The date is unknown (between 1928 and 1930).

In Kyiv, Zerov also continued his scholarly work. He stood at the origin of Ukrainian bibliology, a distinct branch of literature and literary criticism that began to develop after the March revolution

---

29   Panchenko, *Kiltsia na derevi*, 125.

of 1917. The revolution resulted in the emergence of Ukraine as an independent state, and new cultural and bibliology institutions were established, including the first Ukrainian organ of bibliology—the periodical *Knyhar* (Bookseller), published by the Kyiv Chas (Time) Publishing House (31 issues from 1917 to 1920). Following Basil Koroliv-Staryi, Zerov became the second chief editor of this publication, shaping the focus of discussions and the content of this periodical that published bibliographical reviews and articles on the theory of bibliography and book publishing in Ukraine.[30]

Zerov survived these stormy revolutionary years, observing frequent and swift power changes in Kyiv that finally fell under Bolshevik rule in 1920.[31] The same year he married Sofiia (Sonia) Loboda whom he met at a student cafeteria in 1912 (also a student, she attended the Higher Courses for Women in Kyiv).[32] The summer of 1920 was difficult for the Zerovs: Mykola contracted typhus, gradually recovering in Kyiv, which had been shaken by political terror and food shortages. Mykola Simashkevych, the director of the socio-economic professional school in the town of Baryshivka of Pereyaslavl district, a former member of the Central Rada and one of Zerov's acquaintances who briefly visited Kyiv, invited Zerov to teach Ukrainian literature, history, and Latin at his school.[33] In 1920, the couple decided to leave for Baryshivka until better times in Kyiv. They returned to Kyiv in 1923 where Zerov was hired as a professor at the Institute of People's Education to teach the history of Ukrainian literature.

30 B. Krawciw, "Survey of Bibliological Research," in *Ukraine: A Concise Encyclopedia*, ed. Volodymyr Kubijovyc, vol. 2 (Toronto, CA: The Ukrainian National Association/University of Toronto Press, 1971), 428–29.

31 For a detailed narrative about this dramatic period in Ukraine's history, see John S. Reshetar, Jr., *The Ukrainian Revolution, 1917–1920: A Study in Nationalism* (Princeton, NJ: Princeton University Press, 1952).

32 Panchenko, *Kiltsia na derevi*, 79, 157.

33 V'iacheslav Briukhovetskyi, *Mykola Zerov: Literaturno-krytychnyi narys* (Kyiv: Radianskyi pysmennyk, 1990), 92.

Courtesy of TsDAMLIMU, fond 28, op. 1, spr. 218, ark. 1.
Mykola Zerov, Sofiia Zerova, and their son Kostiantyn (Kotyk). The precise date is unknown (1928).

In the early and mid-twenties some liberties were possible in Ukraine, and Ukrainian literary scholars and writers engaged in the process of revising the literary canon in Ukrainian literature, known as the Literary Discussion of 1925–1928.[34] They also tried to "update" it by discovering unpublished texts and studying archives, many of which were scattered and not properly organized.[35] Mykola Zerov's contribution to this process was tremendous. As an example, he gave new life to a person who was completely forgotten in Ukraine—Anatolii Svydnytskyi, a gifted Ukrainian poet, an

---

34   On the Literary Discussion, see A. Leites and M. Yashek, *Desiat rokiv ukrainskoi literatury (1917–1927)*, 2 vols (Kyiv: Derzhavne Vydavnytstvo Ukrainy, 1928; repr. Munich, 1986); George S.N. Luckyj, *Literary Politics in the Soviet Ukraine, 1917–1934* (New York: Columbia University Press, 1956); Mykola Khvyliovyi, *The Cultural Renaissance in Ukraine: Polemical Pamphlets, 1925–1926*, trans., ed. with an introduction by Myroslav Shkandrij (Edmonton, CA: CIUS/University of Alberta, 1986); Vitalii Donchyk, ed., *20-i roky: Literaturni dyskusii, polemiky: Literaturno-krytychni statti* (Kyiv: Dnipro, 1991); Myroslav Shkandrij, *Modernists, Marxists, and the Nation: The Ukrainian Literary Discussion of the 1920s* (Edmonton, CA: CIUS, 1992).

35   Vira Aheieva, *Apolohiia modernu: obrys XX viku* (Kyiv: Hrani-T, 2011), 70–71.

archivist of the Kyiv University's archive, and the author of a series of ethnographical essays and of the novel "Liuboratski" that were published after Svydnytskyi's death. [36] The Literary Discussion among Kyiv and Kharkiv intellectuals, echoed in Lviv and later in Prague, was quite intense. The journals *Shliakh* (Pathway) published in Kyiv and *Shliakhy* (Pathways) published in Lviv embraced the ideas of aesthetic modernism, literary innovation and experimentation, which essentially was a rejection of Enlightenment values and traditional literary techniques. The literati grouped together on the basis of their views and visions of the future of Ukrainian literature. For instance, the literary critic Serhii Yefremov adopted the ideas of Ukrainian *narodnytstvo* (populism or neo-populism) that should govern the development of Ukrainian literature

Courtesy of TsDAMLIMU, fond 28, op. 1, spr. 219, ark. 1.
From left to right: Maksym Rylskyi, Mykola Zerov, and Pavlo Fylypovych. The date is unknown (the 1920s).

---

36 Mykola Zerov, "Anatol Svydnytskyi, ioho postat i tvory," in *Vid Kulisha do Vynnychenka: Narysy z novitnioho ukrainskoho pysmenstva* by Mykola Zerov (Kyiv: Kultura, 1929); reprinted in his *Tvory v dvokh tomakh* (Kyiv: Dnipro, 1990), vol. 2, 323–58.

(i.e. individual freedom, national liberation, and "the progressive populist current in content and form").[37] Mykola Zerov, Viktor Petrov (Viktor Domontovych), Pavlo Fylypovych, Mykhailo Drai-Khmara, Maksym Rylskyi, Ananii Lebid, and Oswald Burghardt (Yurii Klen) promoted the ideas of neoclassicism that drew inspiration from the culture and art of classical antiquity. In their view, rooted in the classical traditions and being part of Western European culture, Ukrainian literature should distance itself from mass and low-brow art, and should rather be a production of highly intellectual creativity, making use of themes and images of antiquity. Unlike other groups, the neoclassicists never established a formal association, but they shared cultural and aesthetic values, and an understanding of what new Ukrainian literature should be in the future.[38] The first publication that introduced yet another literary stream, avant-gardist futurism, was the journal *Mystetstvo* (Art), edited by Hnat Mykhailychenko and Mykhail Semenko who argued that futurism in art was "an analogy of socialism in real life," a politicized leftist view that eventually created the foundation for the new proletarian discourse.[39]

Enjoying support from their readers and their fellow writers, the representatives of proletarian culture vigorously criticized neoclassicists for their gravitation toward "antiquated reminiscences," "elitism," and "excessive aesthetics." Inspired by the national and cultural revolution, creative work by proletarian writers seemed to many more important and more critical to Ukraine's future than the attempts of neoclassicists to return to the very concept of literature rooted in classic European literary tradition. For neoclassicists,

---

37   On Yefremov, see three articles by Petro Odarchenko, Yurii Boiko, and Hryhorii Hrabovych in "Do stolittia narodzhennia Serhiia Yefremova," *Suchasnist*, no. 10 (1976): 16–61, available at https://shron2.chtyvo.org.ua/Suchasnist/1976_N10_190.pdf?.

38   Yurii Sheveliov suggested that Ukrainian neoclassicism was the invention of literary criticism in the 1920s: Yurii Sherekh, "Lehenda pro ukrainskyi neokliasytsyzm," in *Porohy i zaporizhzhia: Literatura, mystetstvo, ideolohii*, vol. 1 (Kharkiv: Folio, 1998), 92–139; Anna Bila, *Symvolizm* (Kyiv: Tempora, 2010), 200–01. See an insightful article on Domontovych by Myroslav Shkandrij, "Avant-Gardist versus Neoclassicist: Viktor Domontovych's Early Novels," *Canadian Slavonic Papers* 42, no. 3 (2000): 315–29.

39   Pavlychko, *Teoriia literatury*, 177.

however, it was crystal clear that art and the rhythms of revolutionary drums were incompatible. They believed that the proletarian

Courtesy of TsDAMLIMU, fond 28, op. 1, spr. 218, ark. 2.
Mykola Zerov (standing, right) and unknown individuals. The date is unknown (between 1928 and 1930).

approach to literature was destructive and even fatal. In their view, the modernization of national literature was impossible unless it was informed and nourished by multi-century European cultural traditions. Zerov, for instance, insisted that modern Ukrainian literature would be created through the writers' persistent studies of its roots—European classical primary sources and the baroque influences of the seventeenth and eighteenths centuries. In 1926, he published a book entitled *To the Sources* (Do dzherel/Ad Fontes), in which he argued that Ukrainian writers' efforts should be grounded in comprehensive knowledge (a fountain of knowledge!) of Ukrainian and world literature that might help them master poetic craft and produce work, highly aesthetic and poetic in form and deeply intellectual in content.[40] The Canadian scholar Myroslav

---

40   Mykola Zerov, *Do dzherel: literaturno-krytychni statti* (Kyiv: Slovo, 1926); or Mykola Zerov, *Do dzherel: istorychno-literaturni ta krytychni statti* (Krakiv/Lviv:

Shkandrij has explicated the meaning of the fountain metaphor which signified a source of knowledge for readers in the twenties, as well as a metaphor for art, flamboyant, sparkling, and playful.[41] A fountain of knowledge and creativity, a metaphor that also emerged in many writers' works in the 1920s, seemed to be an implicit parallel to Zerov's rational principles and beliefs in the European ancient heritage as the foundation for the new Ukrainian literature. "By implication [Shkandrij writes], those who are incapable of enjoying the fountain are potentially condemned to a disastrous inflexibility"[42] which, in Zerov's world, meant catastrophic limitations for literature doomed to remain provincial.

This emphasis on a rational approach to creativity is perceptible in the neoclassicists' poetry, being, to a degree, a response to the modernists' excessive emotionality. The neoclassicists accentuated and praised reserve and calm poetry as the "highest achievement" of a writer. [43] In his analysis of Ukrainian neoclassicists' work, Ukrainian scholar Mykhailo Naienko has maintained that the beauty, the plasticity, and the elegance of their poetry (rational and formal features of neoclassicism) were nevertheless augmented by the artists' irrationalism, inspiration, emotions, and a fountain of fantasy, which "generated artistic energy": their texts radiated the "energy of mythological antiquity projected into modernity."[44] Either way, the postulates and the style adopted by Ukrainian neoclassicists, by definition, could not survive in a regimented society created by the Bolsheviks. It took them a decade to annihilate neoclassicism altogether with its founders. Visiting Kharkiv in 1928 at the end of the literary "wars," Zerov playfully wrote in his autobiography that, because of his activities and publications in 1925, he

---

Ukrainske vydavnytstvo, 1943), available at https://diasporiana.org.ua/wp-content/uploads/books/25500/file.pdf.

41   Myroslav Shkandrij, *Russia and Ukraine: Literature and the Discourse of Empire from Napoleonic to Postcolonial Times* (Montreal & Kingston, CA: McGill-Queen's University Press, 2001), 242.

42   Ibid.

43   Pavlychko, *Teoriia literatury*, 196.

44   Mykhailo Naienko, *Khudozhnia literatura Ukrainy: Vid mifiv do modernoi realnosti* (Kyiv: Prosvita, 2008), 757–58.

got into trouble (popav "bez draki v bolshiie zabiiaki").[45] Being un-aware of the GPU designs to neutralize the nationally conscious Ukrainian intelligentsia, Zerov made it onto the GPU's wanted list during the Literary Discussion, and his frivolous 1928 joke fore-shadowed his individual tragedy and the tragedy of the entire gen-eration of Ukrainian writers known today as part of the Executed Renaissance. The Ukrainian writer and a sixtier (shistdesiatnyk) Roman Korohorodskyi has aptly noted that the Soviet secret organs did not forget anything or anyone, being thoroughly systematic in eliminating the crème of the crème of Ukrainian intellectuals.[46] Zerov became one of them. In 1935, he, as well as Fylypovych and Drai-Khmara, was arrested and accused of organizing an anti-So-viet terrorist nationalist organization.

Face to Face With Reality

By 1928, Zerov and other neoclassicists learned to clandestinely ex-press their true attitudes toward the proletarian reality, codifying it in meaningful silences and pauses and skillfully mastering the craft of euphemisms and subtexts.[47] Yet the impossibility of constantly guarding their thoughts and language inevitably politicized the lit-erary discourse, which was closely watched by the chekists. GPU associates also carefully studied the literati's social background, the meaning and content of their published texts and oral speeches, and their general demeanor. The writers' passionate optimism some-what subdued the chekists' vigilantism while melancholy height-ened their suspicion and doubts about the literati's political relia-bility and loyalty to the regime. Rational and optimistic in his work, Zerov seemed to be highly pessimistic in his worldview and per-ceptions of reality, something that quickly became apparent to the GPU. Moreover, Zerov needed medical attention because of his emotional distress, symptomatic of many literary figures of the 1920s–1930s. Zerov's disturbed psychological state was consistent

---

45 See Zerov's 29 May 1928 "Autobiography" in *Sami pro sebe: Avtobiohrafii ukrainskykh mytsiv 1920-kh rokiv*, ed. Raisa Movchan (Kyiv: Klio, 2015), 218–19.
46 Roman Korohorodskyi, *Do bramy svitla: Portrety* (Kyiv: Dukh i litera, 2016), 29.
47 Pavlychko, *Teoriia literatury*, 198.

with that of the Ukrainian writers Mykola Khvyliovyi (the literary pseudonym of Mykola Fitiliov) and Volodymyr Sosiura, people who survived the turbulent years of the early twentieth century and the civil war in Ukraine. The psychological trauma and neurosis that Zerov acquired during the revolutions, wars, and the terror of the first decade of Bolshevik rule resulted in recurrent depression and nervous breakdowns, a condition that prompted him to seek medical assistance. Zerov's depression was also transparent in his writings: in his sonnets, a recurrent image of a ship that after a lengthy and dangerous journey finally finds a safe haven translucently conveyed the poet's concerns, suffering, and emotional instability.[48] In his essays published during the literary "wars," Zerov was quite assertive and emotional, severely criticizing the vulgarity of his proletarian colleagues' verses. The party establishment assessed his literary criticism from a political standpoint, politicizing literary discourse and creating political labels for its participants. Zerov reacted to that by suggesting that the era of political turbulence and the process of politicization it produced amplified the Ukrainian writers' old traumas and the discord among them during the second part of the 1920s.[49] Surveilling Zerov, the GPU was aware of his stance and his psychological condition. In their analysis, he was a "bourgeois hysteric," a "nationalist," and a "politically unreliable element."

---

48   See Yurii Klen, "Spohady pro neoklasykiv," in *Tvory* by Yurii Klen, Vol. 3 (Toronto, CA: Fundatsiia im. Yuriia Klena, 1960), 154.

49   Mykola Zerov, *Tvory v dvokh tomakh: Poezii, perklady*, vol. 2 (Kyiv: Dnipro, 1990), 385.

Courtesy of TsDAMLIMU, fond 28, op. 1, spr. 218, ark. 8.
Mykola Zerov's office. The date is unknown (between 1928 and 1930).

As mentioned earlier, the writers' behavior during the Literary Discussion, the most significant event in the intellectual history of Ukraine in the 1920s, indeed helped the GPU identify Ukrainian cerebral and opinionated "artistocrats" and proletarian independent thinkers. The chekists also realized that the writers' literary discourse was quickly transformed into a political debate about the future of the Ukrainian nation.[50] The slogan "Away from Moscow" (Het vid Moskvy), which has been wrongfully attributed to Khvyliovyi, became quite popular between March and June of 1926 and widely circulated among literary figures in Kharkiv and Kyiv. Although one cannot find this slogan in Khvyliovyi's writings, this sentiment and idea, however, were implicit in his brilliant pamphlets that he published during the Literary Discussion.[51] Khvy-

---

50 Luckyj, *Literary Politics in the Soviet Ukraine, 1917–1934*; Shkandrij, *Modernists, Marxists and the Nation*.
51 On the origin of this slogan, see Volodymyr Panchenko, "Mykola Khvyliovyi: Istoriia lozunga 'Het vid Moskvy!'," *Den*, 10 January 2019, no. 3–4, available at

liovyi was adamant that Ukrainian writers should expand their intellectual horizons beyond the Russian literature that dominated their psyches for centuries, perpetuating their inferiority complex and slave mentality. For the Soviet secret police and for the regime, these unorthodox ideas presented a grave danger: they were equivalents of ideological deviations and ultimately spelled Ukrainian separatism, a treasonous crime that ought to be eradicated. This perception materialized in the secret GPU circular letter "About Ukrainian Separatism," issued on 4 September of the same year by the leaders of Soviet Ukraine's intelligence Karl Karlson, Osher Abugov, and Boris Kozelskii.[52] In this document, the Ukrainian intelligentsia was identified as anti-Soviet, chauvinistic, and nationalistic, with great potential to shape the Ukrainian peasantry's hateful attitudes towards Soviet power. The authors of this circular letter mentioned Khvyliovyi, suggesting that, being a member of Ukraine's Communist Party, he was thoroughly worked on by the chauvinistic and nationalistic circles in Ukraine and beyond.[53] They outlined several measures on combatting Ukrainian nationalism and separatism that included all-pervasive surveillance of Ukraine's leadership, Ukrainian intellectuals, and their connections, as well as their influence on the Ukrainian peasantry.[54]

In the eyes of the GPU, the close relationship between Khvyliovyi and Zerov that they established in 1923, as well as their correspondence that linked two intellectual spaces in Ukraine, Kharkiv and Kyiv, placed these two prominent writers in the same category of Ukrainian nationalists. Likely, their letters were perlustrated that provided the GPU with the unique opportunity to learn more about Zerov's quite frank thoughts that he shared with

---

https://day.kyiv.ua/ru/article/ukraincy-chitayte/mykola-khvylevyy-istoriya-lozunga-get-vid-moskvi.

52   See the text of the document in Yurii Shapoval, Volodymyr Prystaiko, Vadym Zolotariov, eds., *ChK-GPU-NKVD v Ukraini: Osoby, Fakty, Dokumenty* (Kyiv: Abrys, 1997), 254–67.

53   Ibid., 263–64.

54   Ibid., 266.

Khvyliovyi.[55] Similarly, Khvyliovyi's letters to Zerov were almost confessional, in which he discussed his neuroses and mental instability, and sang praises to Zerov for his remarkable role in shaping Ukrainian literature grounded in European traditions and the traditions of the old Ukrainian intelligentsia.[56] Quite possibly, the intellectual exchange and correspondence between Zerov and Khvyliovyi lasted until Khvyliovyi's death in 1933, yet the only letters that survived the GPU purges are dated from 1923 to 1926. On 13 May 1933, unable to tolerate Soviet censorship, the arrests of his innocent fellow writers, and state violence in the Ukrainian countryside, Khvyliovyi committed suicide in his apartment in the Writers' Home "Slovo" in Kharkiv. On the same day, a few hours after the tragedy, the GPU thoroughly searched Khvyliovyi's apartment and confiscated his private archive.[57] Two years later, immediately after Zerov's arrest, the agency expropriated his private archive, letters, and documents.[58]

Before that there had been several agonizing years for Zerov: the June 1926 Plenum of the Central Committee of Ukraine's Communist Party issued a directive that largely condemned the activities of neoclassicists, which meant that Zerov (as well as his colleagues) could not publish any of his works. For the party, looking up to Europe and placing Ukrainian literature in the context of European cultural traditions constituted an anti-Soviet and nationalist approach.[59] Party officials demanded political loyalty, and in February-March of 1930 Zerov was forced to participate in a show trial,

---

55   Ukrainian writers were aware of the GPU's lustration tactics. See Yurii Shapoval, ed., *Poliuvannia na Valdshnepa: Rozsekrechenyi Mykola Khvyliovyi* (Kyiv: Tempora, 2009), 75.

56   Raisa Movchan, *Ukrainskyi modernism 1920-kh: Portret v istorychnomu inter'ieri* (Kyiv: Stylos, 2008), 35–36.

57   Shapoval, ed., *Poliuvannia na Valdshnepa*, 36.

58   Serhii Bilokin, "Mykola Zerov," *Personalnyi sait istoryka Ukrainy*, https://www. s-bilokin.name/Personalia/Zerov/10.html; Serhii Bilokin, *Masovyi teror iak zasib derzhavnoho upravlinnia v SRSR* (Kyiv: NANU/Kyivske Naukove tovarystvo im. Petra Mohyly, 1999), 42–43.

59   Olha Nikolenko, "Solovetskyi v'iazen Mykola Zerov," *Ridnyi krai*, no. 2 (2010): 160 (150–166), available at http://www.irbis-nbuv.gov.ua/cgi-bin/irbis_nbuv /cgiirbis_64.exe?I21DBN=LINK&P21DBN=UJRN&Z21ID=&S21REF=10&S21 CNR=20&S21STN=1&S21FMT=ASP_meta&C21COM=S&2_S21P03=FILA=&2 _S21STR=Almpolt_2010_2_35.

known as the SVU trial, against the representatives of the Ukrainian
"old intelligentsia." A cascade of arrests among Ukrainian intellectuals, Khvyliovyi's suicide, the death of his 10-years-old son Kostiantyn (Kotyk) from scarlet fever, and the loss of his professorship
at the university in the spring of 1934 devastated Zerov. His intimate life was also in ruins. His wife Sonia fell in love with his friend
Viktor Petrov and she was no longer faithful to Zerov. He suffered
enormously but his love for his only son prevented him from leaving Sonia. Zerov's platonic romance with a Ph.D. student from the
Kharkiv University, Liudmyla Kurylova whom he met in Crimea
in 1926, had no future. She was also married (to a Kharkiv linguist)
and, after Zerov intensely but obliquely confessed his feelings to
Liudmyla, they both agreed not to return to this conversation.[60] Beyond the fact that the authorities left him without any means of survival after terminating his professorship, his intimate tragedy was
another reason why on 11 January 1935 Zerov left Kyiv for Moscow
alone, without his wife.[61]

Zerov's decision was made on an impulse to escape from the
inevitable, the regime's terror, but he still hoped to "resurrect" his
career and to publish his translations. Valentin Asmus, a Moscow
professor, Russian philosopher, literary critic, and a former Kyivite
specializing in the history of ancient and western European philosophy, commissioned Zerov to translate Horace's "The Art of Poetry" (De arte poetica). Zerov even managed to find some job in the
film administration in Moscow, but on 27 April 1935 he was arrested in Pushkino, a town near Moscow where he rented a room
in an accountant's house, and convoyed to Kyiv.[62] It appears that
for the quite cynical chekists the choice of the day of Zerov's arrest
was hardly accidental, a symbolic gift for Zerov's birthday. He
turned 45 a few days before his arrest. The very next day Zerov was

60 Volodymyr Panchenko, *Povist pro Mykolu Zerova* (Kyiv: Dukh i litera, 2018), 453–59.
61 Panchenko, *Povist pro Mykolu Zerova*, 573.
62 Serhii Bilokin, "Mykola Zerov," *Personalnyi sait istoryka Ukrainy*, https://www.s-bilokin.name/Personalia/Zerov/10.html; Panchenko, *Povist pro Mykolu Zerova*, 580–82.

delivered to the Kharkiv GPU headquarters where the interrogator Bondarenko immediately began to work on him.

A comparative analysis of Zerov's interrogation protocols suggests that Bondarenko (and later Litman and other interrogators) heavily modified the original hand-written protocols and Zerov's testimonies. In their typed versions, the statements appeared to be even more self-incriminatory than that which had been beaten out of Zerov in the first place. For example, in the 29 June 1935 protocol, Zerov allegedly stated: "I am also considering myself guilty because for a number of years I was closely working with nationalists [...] sharing their views."[63] Yet in a typed version of this protocol, the word "fully" was added before "sharing," and these semantics certainly amplified Zerov's crime. Long before his arrest, Zerov was aware of the chekists' violence and methods they adopted torturing the accused. Vadym Simashkevych (a son of Mykola Simashkevych, the director of the social-economic school in Baryshivka where Zerov was teaching in the early twenties) was arrested and severely beaten by the chekists. They eventually let Vadym go, but he died at home from his injuries.[64] There is no doubt that Zerov was beaten and psychologically abused during the "investigation." We do not how his glasses were broken, but from his correspondence, we learn that he was forced to endure a lengthy and humiliating bureaucratic procedure to obtain a new pair of glasses.[65]

The multivolume criminal file of Ukrainian intellectuals Mykola Zerov, Ananii Lebid, Pavlo Fylypovych, Marko Voronyi, Leonid Mytkevych, and Borys Pylypenko includes a myriad of interrogation protocols completed by more than a dozen intelligence officers, but what they have in common are similar, almost identical, rhetorical tools employed over and over again, aimed at the complete destruction of the identity and the psyche of the accused.[66]

---

63   HDA SBU (The Sectoral State Archive of the Security Service in Ukraine), f. fp48570, t. 1, ark. 4. See also Bilokin, *Masovyi terror*, 52.
64   Sofiia Zerova, "Spohady pro Mykolu Zerova," Slovo i chas, no. 2 (1996), 78. See also Bilokin, *Masovyi terror*, 224–25.
65   Natalia Kuziakina, *Traiektorii dol* (Kyiv: Tempora, 2010), 584.
66   HDA SBU, f. 6, spr. fp48570.

During their interrogations, the chekists routinely dwelled on the issue of collectivization, requesting information about how the Ukrainian intelligentsia assessed Soviet practices in their private conversations. Their questions included the quotations obtained from their informers who allegedly overheard phrases, such as the "destructive force of collectivization," "the famine that suppresses the Ukrainian nation," and the like. These questions shaped a certain direction and context of the discussion to which the accused were supposed to contribute. Combined with humiliation and physical torture, these tactics were effectively used against Zerov who, after two months, succumbing to the chekists' pressure, expressed his negative attitudes toward Soviet collectivization that "disoriented" him and shaped his nationalistic views. [67] The chekists typically drew a conclusion themselves, asking Zerov to confirm it: "So, because of the famine, frustrated and disillusioned, you decided to act and organized an anti-Soviet nationalist fascist organization, correct?" According to interrogation protocols, the peak of the famine (the spring of 1933) and state repression against Ukrainian nationalists provoked severe depression in Zerov, Rylskyi, and the Ukrainian professor and writer Ananii Lebid. They were forced to admit that they wholeheartedly shared Zerov's feelings and views, conspiring against the state.[68] The chekists allocated the role of the "leader" of a counterrevolutionary organization they allegedly created to Zerov. Zerov finally "confessed" that his organization chose terror as a method against the Communist party leadership, and assassinations were planned against the party leaders Pavlo Postyshev and Stanislav Kosior. During the process of cross examination, Zerov looked doomed: he was crying, confirming the interrogators' insinuations.[69] His confession about a larger plot discussed with other Ukrainian intellectuals — Ukraine's break

---

67   HDA SBU, f. 6, spr. fp48570, vol. 1, ark. 164–65; see also Yaryna Tsymbal, ed., *Spravy dvadtsiatykh: Ukrainskyi avanhard v arhivakh komunistychnykh spetssluzhb* (Lviv: HAD SBU/Tsentr doslidzhen vyzvolnoho rukhu, 2021), 11.

68   HDA SBU, f. 6, spr. fp48570, vol. 1, ark. 165–71,176, 200; Olga Bertelsen, *In the Labyrinth of the KGB: Ukraine's Intelligentsia in the 1960s–1970s* (New York: Lexington Books, 2022), ch. 5.

69   Panchenko, *Povist pro Mykolu Zerova*, 594–598.

from the USSR with the help of fascist states — became the culmination of his depositions which sealed his fate.[70] The pressure and special interrogation techniques broke many Ukrainian intellectuals. They denounced their friends and cried and begged their tormentors for forgiveness. Ananii Lebid, part of the case fabricated against Zerov, was among the few who withstood the chekists' tortures and refused to agree to scenarios proposed by his interrogators about a counterrevolutionary organization that allegedly existed in Ukraine.[71]

Sentenced to ten years in labor camps,[72] Zerov asked his wife Sonia to sell a collection of Pushkin's works, part of his extensive library, to be able to purchase necessary items for his survival in camps. The family had no savings, and the sale of the library that belonged to one of the most prominent literary scholars in Ukraine had begun. Later Zerov thanked his wife for that, considering himself fortunate while observing a lack of personal belongings among other prisoners.[73]

On 31 June 1936, Zerov, suffering from furunculosis, finally arrived at the Solovky where he spent the last year and five months of his life.[74] He found himself in the company of the writers, scholars, and actors Pavlo Florenskyi, Myroslav Irchan, Oleksa Slisarenko, Hryhorii Epik, Vasyl Mysyk, Leonid Mytkevych, and Les Kurbas. Zerov was assigned to clean the camp facilities. After his working day, he was allowed to use the guard's room where he was working on his translations. It came as a surprise to Zerov that there was a library in the Solovky where he could find fresh periodicals and books. Eventually, he was appointed as a librarian

70   HDA SBU, f. 6, spr. 48570-FP, vol. 1, ark. 232.
71   Bertelsen, In the Labyrinth of the KGB, ch. 5.
72   Petro Kulakovskyi, Heorhii Smirnov, and Yurii Shapoval, eds., Ostannia adresa, t. 1 (Kyiv: Sluzhba Bezpeky Ukrainy/Sfera, 1997), 38.
73   S. A. Halchenko and V. P. Saienko, eds., Natalia Kuziakina: Avtoportret, interv'iu, publikatsii riznykh lit (Drohobych, Kyiv, Odesa: VF "Vidrodzhennia," 2010), 341. See also Zerov's letters in TsDAMLIMu, f. 28, op. 1, no. 153; V. O. Tolstov, ed., "Z lystuvannia M. K. Zerova," Radianske literaturoznavstvo, no. 1 (325) (1988): 48–68; and no. 4 (328), 33–49.
74   Panchenko, Povist pro Mykolu Zerova, 600. The Solovky prison camp was established in 1923 on the Solovetskyi Island in the White Sea for the opponents of the Bolshevik regime.

there.[75] He was in heaven, although lamenting that he could not be self-sufficient. Sonia was still sending him some money, so that Zerov could supplement the camp's poor diet. He wrote to her: "Sadly, of course, I am still sitting on your neck, but what can I do? I have no idea how I can get out of this situation."[76]

The state solved this dilemma for Zerov. On 3 November 1937, he was shot in the back of his head, like another 1,111 people who were brought with him from the Solovky camp, and buried in a mass grave in Sandarmokh, Karelia.[77] Yet the lies that placed Zerov in the Solovky continued after his murder. The GPU not only fabricated individual and collective criminal cases against innocent people but also falsified information about the prisoners' executions, informing their relatives about their dearest's death that allegedly occurred from natural causes. This became common practice during the Great Terror in 1937–1938 to camouflage mass killings and mislead devastated relatives, the "truth-seekers."[78] In early June 1938 the authorities stopped accepting money transfers, parcels, and books that Sonia regularly sent to her husband. Both Zerov's father and Sonia made inquiries about Zerov, and received contradictory responses from the authorities.[79] Before the war, Zerov's father was informed that Mykola passed away in April of 1937 at a hospital and, after the war, Sonia was provided another date of Zerov's death: he allegedly died of heart failure on 13 October 1941.[80] At the height of the first wave of rehabilitation campaigns[81] on 26 November 1958, Zerova wrote to the Military Tribunal of the Kyiv Military District, requesting a document about the precise

---

75 Semen Pidhainyi, "Mykola Zerov," in Ostannia adresa, eds. Petro Kulakovskyi and Yurii Shapoval, t. 3 (Kyiv: Sluzhba Bezpeky Ukrainy/Sfera, 1999), 371.

76 Halchenko and Saienko, 343; Panchenko, Povist pro Mykolu Zerova, 603.

77 Yurii Dmitriev, Mesto pamiati Sandarmokh, ed. Anatolii Razumov (Petrozavodsk: Memorial, 2019), 320, 367, 431.

78 Bilokin, Masovyi terror, 54–55.

79 Sofiia Zerova, "Spohady pro Mykolu Zerova," in Vybrani tvory by Mykola Zerov, ed. Volodymyr Panchenko (Kyiv: Smoloskyp, 2015), 698–99.

80 Tsymbal, Spravy dvadtsiatykh, 11.

81 For more details on post-Stalin rehabilitation campaigns, see A. N. Yakovlev et al., eds., Reabilitatsiia: Kak eto bylo. Mart 1953–Fevral 1956 gg., available at Tsentr istoricheskoi pamiati/Permskaia regionalnaia blagotvoritelnaia obshchestvennaia organizatsiia, http://pmem.ru/index.php?id=154.

term that her husband served in labor camps. Three days later, she received a response from the Deputy Head of the Military Tribunal Colonel of Justice M. Kozlov, in which he informed Zerova that her husband was sentenced to death by the directive of the Special Troika of the UNKVD in Leningrad oblast and was shot on 3 November 1937.[82]

The short-lived Thaw and re-Stalinization stagnated the process of rehabilitation, and the secret police returned to its habitual modus operandi, lies, and violence that continued to take the lives of Ukrainian writers and intellectuals until the very end of the Soviet Union. More fundamentally, these lies and violence perpetuated the cultural amnesia among the Ukrainians who, through enormous political obstacles and linguistic difficulties, began to discover the works published by Zerov and other Ukrainian intellectuals only in independent Ukraine.

Epilogue

Zerov had a passion for life and a strong wish to live a life of the mind. But his origin, style, tone, and behavior were drastically inconsistent with the Bolshevik ideal of a Soviet intellectual, a domesticated proletarian who was supposed to communicate Communist slogans and formulas prescribed by the state. In fact, Zerov was the opposite of this ideal, and could not possibly survive one of the bloodiest GPU operations in Stalinist Ukraine—the slaughter of millions of people in the 1920s and 1930s. Devising a nationalist conspiracy in Ukraine, GPU operatives engaged in an ethnic cleansing operation, attempting to solve the Ukrainian question once and for all by changing the ethnic composition of the republic and eliminating Ukrainian culture. The persistence of these efforts can be traced in criminal files from 1932 to 1938 that have been preserved in the former KGB archives in Ukraine, including Zerov's group criminal file. The very existence of people like Zerov, as well as the national cultural institutions and projects they established and

---

82 Serhii Bilokin, "Mykola Zerov," *Personalnyi sait istoryka Ukrainy*, https://www.s-bilokin.name/Personalia/Zerov/10.html; see also Panchenko, *Povist pro Mykolu Zerova*, 604.

were part of (national encyclopedias, committees on Ukrainian spelling, linguistics and history, theatres and university departments), was associated with nationalism and ultimately separatism, and had to be destroyed. By the mid-thirties, the Ukrainian cultural landscape had become one dimensional and flat, and by the end of this decade, almost all Ukrainian institutions were closed, modified and restructured with a greater orientation toward their essential russification. The repression of cultural figures in Ukraine in the 1930s affected thousands. In arresting "terrorists" like Zerov in Ukraine who allegedly were organized in groups to demolish Soviet power in the republic, the secret police functioned almost exclusively as the agency that eliminated political opposition to the regime. Like all genocides, all GPU operations in Ukraine aimed at eliminating the nationally conscious elites were conducted secretly, which significantly impeded the return of Zerov's writings to his readers and problematized the Ukrainians' societal awareness of the legacies of the Executed Renaissance.[83]

Interrogation rooms and prison confronted Zerov in a violent and barbaric way. The general atmosphere of violence that reigned in the secret organs in the 1930s encouraged the sadistic personalities of those who worked there. Arresting people on their birthdays, executing people on New Year's Eve, and often working in blood up to their ankles, many GPU agents seemed to take special pleasure from their sadistic actions. "Nationalists" like Zerov were severely beaten and tortured by their interrogators. The outcome of a decade of terror in Ukraine was rather predictable. Whoever among Ukrainian intellectuals was left in Ukraine after 1933 were shot during the Great Terror of 1937–1938, including those who were in labor camps. Criminal cases of those who served their lengthy sentences in the Solovky were reopened, and they were shot as Ukrainian nationalists.[84] Just a few survived the terror. For many and, perhaps, also for Zerov, Sandarmokh became a place of liberation:

---

83 On the concealment and denial of Soviet genocidal practices in Ukraine in the 1920s and 1930s, see Malko, The *Ukrainian Intelligentsia and Genocide*.

84 Most of them were shot on 3 November 1937 in Sandarmokh, Karelia by the GB captain Matveev.

death ended their suffering and the violence to which they had been subjected for a decade.

Zerov's remains cannot be accurately located or identified because he shared a grave with thousands of other cultural figures, such as Les Kurbas. They were buried together in the frozen soil of Karelia in pits dug by their fellow prisoners. Yet Sandarmokh is not only a place where their remains are resting. It also became a burial place of these people's ideas, novels, poems, and theatre performances that have never been and will never be consummated. These ideas are irrevocably lost, without having had the opportunity to be born. Their artistic dreams and goals remained unattainable, and this loss is irredeemable. During the period of one decade, the terror tore a hole in the fabric of Ukrainian culture that has never been and may never be mended. The anti-Ukrainian, anti-human, anti-aesthetic and anti-intellectual nature of the Soviet Communist regime and its faithful servants is evident in thousands of criminal cases fabricated by the regime to eliminate the nationally conscious intelligentsia in Ukraine. The beautiful and subtle was doomed, and the crude and unsophisticated was encouraged and promoted.

Many scholars have suggested that Stalin's repressions turned the graphical representation of the genealogical tree of most Ukrainian intellectuals' families upside down. Many families were completely obliterated and others lost most of their members. Zerov left no off-spring, but he and his writings have certainly nurtured many pupils, inspiring them to write. Their works, together with the ones of the Executed Renaissance that survived the Soviet purges, expand the space of our memory, as well as our knowledge about ethnocide and the enormous cultural disruption in Ukraine in the 1920s and 1930s and the individual contributions of people like Zerov to Ukrainian literature and culture.

The Executed Renaissance
The Ukrainian Intelligentsia in the 1920s and 1930s

Victoria Malko

A constellation of literary talent and vanguard thinkers in the 1920s and 1930s could have filled a century with their masterpieces, securing a place for Ukraine in the heart of European civilization. These decades were the apotheosis of national self-realization, a burst of energy after centuries of oppression by imperial Russian rulers. Alas, the renaissance of the Ukrainian language, literature, and art that released energy of innovative experimentation was brutally curtailed by the repressive apparatus of the totalitarian system. The "red renaissance" nipped the Ukrainian culture in the bud in the 1930s. The Ukrainian renaissance was soaked in blood of the repressed, whose biographies ended with the date of the execution, exile, or suicide. Those who survived could not create as freely as they dared. The era was poignantly described by Polish publicist, Jerzy Giedroyc, in his letter to Ukrainian literature researcher Yuri Lavrinenko,[1] who later used it as the title for a collection of that generation's best literary works—"executed renaissance."[2] The metaphor, borrowed from an anthology of works published between 1917 and 1933, highlights the tragic beauty of verses and novels that

---

1   Yuri Lavrinenko (1905–1987) was a literary scholar, critic, and publicist. In 1930, after graduation from the Kharkiv Institute of People's Education, he completed a doctorate at the Institute of Literature of the Academy of Sciences of the Ukrainian SSR. He was arrested several times between 1933 and 1935, and from 1935 to 1939 he was imprisoned in a concentration camp in Norilsk, Russia. He was exiled after his release. During World War II, he became a refugee in a Displaced Persons camp in Germany. In 1950, he emigrated to the United States. In 1955–1960, together with Ivan Koshelivets, he edited *Ukraïnska literaturna hazeta* (Ukrainian Literary Newspaper). He published the anthology *Rozstriliane vidrodzhennia* (The Executed Renaissance) in 1959.

2   Yuri Lavrinenko, *Rozstriliane vidrodzhennia: Antolohiia, 1917–1933* (The Executed Renaissance: An Anthology, 1917–1933) (Kyïv: Smoloskyp, 2004).

fascinated generations of readers. It commemorates fearlessness of
the creative genius in the time of darkness for speaking the truth.

The first decades of the twentieth century brought war, revolution, and short-lived independence of Ukraine. Bolshevik leader
Vladimir Lenin, while recognizing the independent Ukrainian National Republic (UNR), issued an ultimatum and ordered the Red
Army to invade.[3] Lenin's theses on the Russian Communist Party's
policy toward Ukraine, drafted in November 1919, established a
blueprint for denationalization, demilitarization, and decapitation
of Ukraine's national elites.[4] The Red Terror[5] and the famine of
1921–1923 subdued the national liberation struggle. This meant that
Ukraine was partitioned between Romanian, Czech, Polish, and
Russian occupational authorities. By 1923, the Ukrainian Foreign
Office was liquidated. As Nataliia Polonska-Vasylenko noted, "the
history of the Ukrainian emigration emerged under the yoke of foreign occupation, the struggle for one's national identity, culture,
and freedom."[6]

The Ukrainian government-in-exile missions in Paris, Warsaw, and Prague carried out the mission to unite Ukrainian intellectual elites and remnants of the UNR army to keep the flame of
independence alive. They raised their voices to protest Bolshevik
occupation and political repressions.[7] In November 1927, leaders of

---

3   Lenin issued the ultimatum in December 1917. The first Russian invasion and
     occupation of Ukraine lasted from January to April 1918, the second—from
     January to August 1919, and the third started in December 1919.
4   "Draft Theses of the Central Committee of the Russian Communist Party
     (Bolsheviks) Concerning Policy in the Ukraine," in Richard Pipes, ed., *The
     Unknown Lenin: From the Secret Archive* (New Haven: Yale University Press,
     1996), 76–77.
5   The Red Terror was a period of repressions and mass killings carried out by the
     Cheka beginning in 1918, against political enemies of the Bolsheviks. In Soviet
     Ukraine, the system of Bolshevik extrajudicial killings included two methods:
     summary executions of randomly selected civilians accused of harboring or
     aiding "bandits" (*vidpovidachi*) and hostage taking used to terrorize and disarm
     the countryside (*zaruchnytstvo*).
6   Nataliia Polonska-Vasylenko, *Istoriia Ukraïny, 1900–1923 rr.* (History of
     Ukraine, 1900–1923) (Kyïv: Pam'iatky Ukraïny, 1991), 133.
7   Raïsa Movchan, "Na smertnii hrani" (On the Verge of Death), in *Ukraïna:
     Antolohiia pam'iatok derzhavotvorennia X–XX st.* (Ukraine: An Anthology of
     Remembrances of State Formation in the 10th—20th centuries), 10 vols., vol. 8,
     Rozstriliane vidrodzhennia Ukraïny (1920-ti – 1930-ti roky XX st.) (The Executed

four Ukrainian diaspora organizations gathered at their first conference in Berlin, Germany, followed by their second conference in
April 1928 in Prague, Czechoslovakia. In late January—early February 1929, these organization founded the Organization of Ukrainian Nationalists (OUN) at the first congress in Vienna, Austria.[8]
Most of these gatherings were conspiratorial in nature to evade arrests. During plenary and committee meetings, delegates discussed
ideological, socioeconomic, military, political, cultural, educational,
and organizational matters. The congress concluded its work with
a speech by the newly elected head of the OUN, Yevhen
Konovalets, who spoke eloquently about the choice that the Ukrainians face in a global drama to "either be creators or victims of history." He prophesied that Ukraine will face great challenges on the
road to regaining its independence because "the restoration of
Ukraine's sovereignty is only possible with the liquidation of Moscow's empire," which he believed would "reshape the entire Eastern Europe and larger parts of Asia, and in the end affect the global
political outlook."[9]

Russian Bolsheviks, lacking popular support, needed to win
the Ukrainian intelligentsia on their side because writers, artists,
university professors, teachers, and clergy had enormous influence
on the minds of the local population. The Ukrainian intelligentsia
became a special focus of attention because they did not fit into the
class structure of the society that Bolsheviks were building based
on Marxist principles. In case of Ukraine, as Olha Koliastruk
pointed out, members of the intelligentsia were learned strata of the
society; they came from various social classes—nobility, merchants,

---

Renaissance of Ukraine, 1920s—1930s of the 20th century) (Kyïv: Vyd-vo
Solomiï Pavlychko "Osnovy," 2009), 10.

8   These diaspora organizations included the Ukrainian Military Organization
     (1920), the Ukrainian Nationalist Youth (1922), the League of Ukrainian
     Nationalists (1925), and the Union of Ukrainian Nationalist Youth (1926). For
     more on the structure and history of the Organization of Ukrainian
     Nationalists, see Ivan Patryliak, *Vyzvolna borotba OUN i UPA (1939–1960):
     Monohrafiia* (The Liberation Struggle of the OUN and UPA, 1939–1960: A
     Monograph) (Kyïv: VD ADEF-Ukraïna, 2020) and Petro Mirchuk, *Narys istoriï
     OUN, 1920–1939* (An Essay on the History of the OUN, 1920–1939) (Kyïv:
     Ukraïnska vydavnycha spilka, 2007).

9   Mirchuk, *Narys istoriï OUN*, 77.

village parish priests, and students.[10] Most of the Ukrainian intelligentsia had roots in the countryside as they were sons and daughters of the clergy. Through social engineering Bolsheviks subverted Ukraine's intellectual and cultural elites and forced them to work for the regime.[11] Leon Trotsky put it bluntly: "We will use hunger to force the intelligentsia to work for us."[12]

The task of the Russian Communist Party's policy toward Ukraine was to overcome its complete dependence on "old intelligentsia" and train "red professors" and loyal cadres that could be one hundred percent "Soviet" to carry out various campaigns without opposition to the regime. Moscow's rulers pursued an ambiguous nationality policy as a compromise with local elites to root Soviet ideology among the colonized population.[13] Introduced in 1923 at the Twelfth Congress of the Russian Communist Party, this policy known as korenizatsiia[14] (or Ukrainization in the Ukrainian republic of the newly created Union of Soviet Socialist Republics in territories of the former Russian Empire) envisioned cultural national autonomy plus training of loyal cadres proficient in the language of the local population. Some Western scholars still continue to argue that Ukrainization was an affirmative action policy that allowed indigenous cultures to flourish.[15] They still believe in this

10   Olha Koliastruk, *Intelihentsiia USRR u 1920-ti roky: povsiakdenne zhyttia* (Intelligentsia of the Ukrainian SSR in the 1920s: Everyday Life) (Kharkiv: "Rarytety Ukraïny," 2010).

11   Victoria A. Malko, *The Ukrainian Intelligentsia and Genocide: The Struggle for History, Language, and Culture in the 1920s and 1930s* (Lanham: Lexington Books, 2021).

12   Quoted in V. Topolianskii, *Vozhdi v zakone: Ocherki fiziologii vlasti* (Leaders in Law: Essays on the Physiology of Power) (Moscow: Izd-vo "Prava cheloveka," 1996), 25.

13   Elena Borisenok, *Fenomen Sovetskoi ukrainizatsii* (A Phenomenon of Soviet Ukrainization) (Moscow: Evropa, 2006).

14   Giuseppe Perri, "*Korenizacija*: an Ambiguous and Temporary Strategy of Legitimization of Soviet Power in Ukraine (1923–1933) and Its Legacy," *History of Communism in Europe*, no. 5 (2014): 131–154. Francine Hirsch defined Soviet nationality policy to be "*by its nature* both a creative and a destructive process." See Francine Hirsch, "Race without the Practice of Racial Politics," *Slavic Review* 61, no. 1 (2002): 42.

15   Terry Martin, *The Affirmative Action Empire: Nations and Nationalism in the Soviet Union, 1923–1939* (Cornell University Press, 2001); Ronald Grigor Suny and Terry Martin, eds., *A State of Nations: Empire and Nation-Making in the Age of*

Soviet myth of sovereignty and sustainability of ethnic cultures in constituent republics. In fact, the policy served to consolidate one-party rule over the multitude of groups that comprised the "prison of nations." The purpose of such policy was to placate and harness liberation movements. As Hiroaki Kuromiya stated, the policy "at least partially was able to contain the explosive nature of national ideology."[16]

The rhetoric behind Ukrainization masked the real goal of removing those who believed in cultural distinctiveness and national statehood, an approach that Yuri Shapoval called "double bookkeeping."[17] In November 1923, a secret circular from Moscow instructed its local GPU[18] offices to establish total control over professors, lecturers, and students, their activities in associations, meetings, and publications, by installing a network of informers to report about public sentiments, private comments, and anti-Soviet

Lenin and Stalin (New York: Oxford University Press, 2001); Matthew D. Pauly, *Breaking the Tongue: Language, Education, and Power in Soviet Ukraine, 1923-1934* (Toronto: University of Toronto Press, 2014).

16 Hiroaki Kuromiya, *Freedom and Terror in the Donbas: The Ukrainian-Russian Frontier, 1870-1990* (Cambridge: Cambridge University Press, 1998), 203.

17 Yuri Shapoval, *Ukraïna 20–50-kh rokiv: storinky nenapysanoï istoriï* (Ukraine in the 1920s–1950s: Pages of an Unwritten History) (Kyïv: Naukova dumka, 1993), 26.

18 The GPU (in Russian *Gosudarstvennoe politicheskoe upravlenie*), or State Political Directorate, was a successor of Cheka, the All-Russian Extraordinary Commission for Combatting Counterrevolution, Speculation, Sabotage, and Misuse of Authority, colloquially known as VChK (*Vserossiiskaia chrezvychainaia komissiia po borbe s kontrrevoliutsiei i sabotazhem*). Officials of the Cheka were known as chekists. From 1922 to 1934, the GPU (Ukrainian abbreviation DPU) was a special organ of the Bolshevik occupational regime in Soviet Ukraine, which carried out political repressions, executions, arrests, and deportations. In 1928, the GPU was granted the right to conduct trials without prosecutor's consent. In 1929, the so-called *troika* were instituted to expedite the prosecution of legal cases. In 1932-1933, the GPU oversaw the implementation of the law on the "protection of socialist property" (known as the "five ears of wheat" law) and conducted arrests, deportations, and executions of all those who were charged for violating the law by gleaning kernels of wheat in the fields. The Ukrainian branch of the GPU was taken over by Moscow on August 13, 1924. It had never been independent; thus, cadre policies were dictated by Moscow. See Yuri Shapoval, Volodymyr Prystaiko, and Vadym Zolotariov, *ChK-GPU-NKVD v Ukraïni: Osoby, fakty, dokumenty* (ChK-GPU-NKVD in Ukraine: Personalities, Facts, Documents) (Kyïv: Abris, 1997), 9–10.

clandestine activities in Ukraine.[19] In early 1924, the GPU under Josef Stalin's command created a list of "suspected counterrevolutionaries" in Ukraine for further surveillance with subsequent annihilation. The list included a dozen social groups, branded as "secret enemies of the Soviet regime," among them followers of Symon Petliura,[20] the leader of the UNR, labelled "Petliurists," and "nationalists of all shades of opinion."[21] The list also included all scholars and specialists of the "old school," meaning non-Soviet. Although the circular did not prescribe the methods of liquidation, this document is crucial evidence that teachers of the "old school" and professors together with the "Petliurists" were included in the list for extermination as members of the Ukrainian national group. Scholars confirm that Moscow's initial intent was clandestine "counter-Ukrainization."[22]

Perceived "passivity" of the GPU during the New Economic Policy (NEP)[23] era was temporary. As historian Valentyn Moroz

---

19 Vasyl Danylenko, *Ukraïnska intelihentsiia i vlada: Zvedennia sekretnoho viddilu DPU USRR 1927–1929 rr.* (The Ukrainian Intelligentsia and Power: Reports from a Secret Department of the DPU of the Ukrainian SSR, 1927–1929) (Kyïv: Tempora, 2012), 21.

20 Symon Petliura (1879–1926) was a native of Poltava, Ukraine. As a theology student, he joined an underground socialist movement, working as a journalist and editor. For a brief period, he worked as an archivist in the Kuban, studying history of the Ukrainian Cossack settlements in the North Caucasus. He was Secretary of War in the Central Rada (Council), then a member of the Directory and the Commander-in-Chief of the Army of the UNR. He later became the head of the Directory (in May 1919) and head of the Ukrainian government-in-exile (after November 1920). He was assassinated in Paris in May 1926 by a Soviet security police agent.

21 The top-secret circular of February 1924 was signed by the Chief of the Lubny Okruh OGPU Section Dvianinov and Chief of Counterespionage Section Zhukov. The English translation of the circular was published in the *Ukrainian Review* (London) in 1958 (issue 6, 149–150) and reprinted in Robert Conquest, *The Harvest of Sorrow: Soviet Collectivization and the Terror–Famine* (New York: Oxford University Press, 1986), 71–72.

22 Myroslav Shkandrij and Olga Bertelsen, "The Soviet Regime's National Operations in Ukraine, 1929–1934," *Canadian Slavonic Papers* 55, nos. 3–4 (2013): 417–447.

23 The NEP was initiated in 1921, when *prodrazverstka* (expropriation of agricultural produce) was suspended and replaced with a fixed tax, giving farmers the opportunity to sell their produce on the free market. The legalization of the market forced the Bolshevik leaders to allow entrepreneurial activity. Industries were nationalized and organized into trusts based on principles of cost accounting. The

noted, economically prosperous due to the NEP and culturally awakened due to the policy of Ukrainization, the republic presented a threat of political separation from Russia, which would mean a collapse of the communist system.[24] As a secret GPU circular of June 1925 instructed, the political police "should therefore not lose a good opportunity to unmask our enemies, in order to deal them a crushing blow when the time comes."[25] Meanwhile, leading intellectuals, like Mykhailo Hrushevskyi, Stepan Rudnytskyi, Antin Krushelnytskyi, were lured into returning by Bolshevik promises of respectable positions in Soviet Ukraine, whereas the Central Committee of the Communist Party of Ukraine (Bolsheviks) and the GPU held secret meetings on how to deal with intelligentsia. In May 1925, a closed meeting of the Politburo heard a report from the GPU and adopted a resolution to create a commission to examine tactics of dealing with the Ukrainian intelligentsia, especially its Academy of Sciences and Hrushevskyi. The GPU put professor Hrushevskyi under surveillance, while focusing on his influential colleague, academician Serhii Yefremov, in order to subvert Ukrainian intellectual elites.[26]

The policy of Ukrainization was perceived as a "mousetrap"[27] because a good number of intellectuals who had immigrated abroad came back to Ukraine in 1925 at the invitation of the Soviet government. Moscow dispatched "Ukrainian diplomats" Yuri Kotsiubynskyi and Oleksandr Shumskyi as representatives of Soviet

production was revived after the restoration of the credit and banking system, the introduction of a stable currency, and the promotion of cooperative and private enterprises. The policy was curtailed in 1928.

24 Valentyn Moroz, "Nationalism and Genocide: The Origin of the Artificial Famine of 1932–1933 in Ukraine," *The Journal of Historical Review* 6, no. 2 (1985): 207–220.

25 *Ukrainian Review*, no. 6 (1958): 156; quoted in Conquest, *The Harvest of Sorrow*, 71.

26 Volodymyr Prystaiko and Yuri Shapoval, *Mykhailo Hrushevskyi i GPU-NKVD: Trahichne desiatylittia, 1924–1934* (Mykhailo Hrushevskyi and GPU-NKVD: A Tragic Decade, 1924–1934) (Kyïv: "Ukraïna," 1996), 131, 133–134.

27 This observation is supported by contemporaries as intimated by the father of Mykola Kotcherha, who was singing in a folk choir and travelling from villages to towns to perform Ukrainian choral music in concerts (personal communication, September 19, 2019). Mykola Kotcherha is president of the Ukrainian Genocide Famine Foundation in Chicago, Illinois.

Ukraine to the largest diaspora centers in Vienna and Warsaw, respectively, to lure Ukrainian émigré scholars and writers, as well as to extradite Petliura and his generals under an "amnesty," and eventually to put an end to Ukrainian political activities outside the Soviet borders.[28] Some contemporary scholars disagree with the "mousetrap" argument.[29] They agree, though, that most active members of the nationally conscious intelligentsia lured back to Ukraine, among them former leader of the Central Rada historian Mykhailo Hrushevskyi, writer Mykola Voronyi, and the entire family of Antin Krushelnytskyi, later disappeared, were exiled, or executed.

Programmatic Communist Party documents issued at the time tell little about theoretical bases of the policy of Ukrainization.[30] Lazar Kaganovich,[31] Stalin's most reliable trouble-shooter, who mastered the Ukrainian language and oversaw its implementation in Ukraine, did not hide from his comrades that it was a tactical

---

28   See V. Naddniprianets, *Ukraïnski natsional-komunisty: ïkh rolia u vyzvolnii borotbi Ukraïny 1917–1956 rr.* (Ukrainian National-Communists: Their Role in Ukraine's Liberation Struggle, 1917–1956) (Munich: Political Section of the Ukrainian National Guard, 1956), 23.

29   Dmytro Arkhireiskyi and Viktor Chentsov, "Antyradianska natsionalna opozytsiia v USRR v 20-ti rr.: pohliad na problemu kriz arkhivni dzherela" (Anti-Soviet National Opposition in the Ukrainian SSR in the 1920s: A View on the Problem through the Lens of Archival Sources), *Z arkhiviv VUChK, GPU, NKVD, KGB* (From the Archives of VUChK, GPU, NKVD, KGB), no. 2–4 (2000): 30.

30   Yuri Sheveliov, "Ukraïnizatsiia: radianska polityka 1925–1932 rokiv" (Ukrainization: Soviet Policy, 1925–1932), *Suchasnist* (Modernity) 5 (1983): 42.

31   Lazar Kaganovich (1893–1991), born to Jewish parents in the Radomysl district, Kyïv Governorate of the Russian Empire, was the secretary general of the Communist Party (Bolsheviks) of Ukraine from 1925 to 1928 and secretary of the Central Committee of the All-Union Communist Party (Bolsheviks) from 1928 to 1939. In October 1932, he headed an extraordinary grain-procurement commission, which, under the pretext of grain procurement, confiscated all food supplies from farmers in the North Caucasus, especially the Kuban region, thereby condemning them to death from starvation. Along with Josef Stalin, Viacheslav Molotov, Pavel Postyshev, Stanislav Kosior, Vlas Chubar, and Mendel Khataievich, he was accused of perpetrating genocide in Soviet Ukraine in 1932–1933 by a Ukrainian Court of Appeal in January 2010, but criminal proceedings against them were quashed because the accused were already dead.

move.[32] The policy, indeed, was ambiguous. It did not fit into Marxist doctrine of proletarian internationalism. By January 1926, all government employees were required to pass language tests. To get a job or a degree, one had to speak Ukrainian. Yet, 1926 became a turning point. In March of that year, a pamphlet "On Ukrainian Society" was circulated among the GPU personnel. In May, Petliura was assassinated in Paris by Samuil Schwartzbard. In August, Metropolitan Vasyl Lypkivskyi, who headed the Ukrainian Autocephalous Orthodox Church (UAOC), and had been known as a "secret propagator of Ukrainian separatism," was arrested.[33] In September of that year, another GPU circular "On Ukrainian Separatism" spelled out goals, forms, and methods of fighting against a "tendency to separate Ukraine from Russia."[34] In October, five months after Petliura's murder, a propaganda film was released under an acronym PKP, decoded as "Piłsudski Bought Petliura," aiming to denounce the Ukrainian national leader as a traitor and Piłsudski's agent.[35]

Even in far-away Paris, Petliura as the leader of Ukraine's government-in-exile presented a formidable threat to Stalin. Comparing the Bolsheviks to the Conquistadors, Petliura characterized Soviet "Ukrainization" as a typical colonial policy, where colonizers are required to master the indigenous language of the colonized to

---

32   See Kaganovich's speech at the Tenth Congress of the Communist Party (Bolsheviks) of Ukraine, November 1927, in *Budivnytstvo Radianskoï Ukraïny: Zbirnyk* (The Construction of Soviet Ukraine: A Collection of Documents), vyp. 1 (Kharkiv: DVU), 150; cited in Sheveliov, "Ukraïnizatsiia."

33   Conquest, *The Harvest of Sorrow*, 210–211.

34   Danylenko, *Ukraïnska intelihentsiia i vlada*, 25. For the analysis and the text of the document, see Yuri Shapoval, "'On Ukrainian Separatism': A GPU Circular of 1926," *Harvard Ukrainian Studies* 18, no. 3–4 (1994): 275–302.

35   The transcript for the movie was written by Heorhii Stabovyi and Yakov Livshits in 1926. Balytskyi forced to cut the movie, giving as a reason that GPU methods could be revealed. A film poster, designed by A. Finohenov, depicts the Red Cavalry in pursuit of surviving soldiers of Yurko Tiutiunnyk's army. In the center of the poster, Hryhorii Kotovskyi crosses off a golden Trident on a blue background with his sword. The image amplifies the concept that Bolsheviks in Ukraine are successors of the Ukrainian National Republic (UNR). See Lubomyr Hosejko, *Ukrainian Film Poster of the 1920s: VUFKU* (Kyïv: Oleksandr Dovzhenko National Center, 2015), 19, 21, 34–35, 39, 58–59. See the film poster at https://vufku.org/lost/p-k-p/.

create an illusion that rapacious extraction of resources is carried out not by the foreign power, but by the "brothers" who "speak our language."[36] Deconstructing a speech Vlas Chubar[37] addressed to the Communist Youth League in April 1926, Petliura summed up Soviet nationality policy as a failure. Articulating his idea that the pro-Moscow orientation means political and cultural suicide for Ukraine, Petliura dubbed the Bolsheviks' policy "catching of Ukrainian souls." He warned: "The [Soviet] government can transport trainloads of Ukrainian bread, sugar, coal, all of Ukraine's riches, except her Ukrainian soul."[38] Petliura called Chubar a representative of the illegal occupational regime and his speech aimed at the younger generation of Ukrainians as an attempt to train new Janissaries. The following month, on May 25, 1926, Petliura was assassinated by an agent of the Soviet security police on his way to a meeting of Ukrainian émigré organizations in Paris. The news like an arrow broke the hearts of the Ukrainian intelligentsia: "It felt like the earth was splitting apart... it meant the head was severed from the body of the nation. How will Ukraine exist without its head? Who will lead?"[39]

The Ukrainization was resisted by communist bosses dispatched to the republic and by parents of Russian-speaking chil-

---

36   Symon Petliura, "'Rosiiska menshist' na Ukraïni (z pryvodu dyskusiï na ostannii sesiï VTsIK-a)" (The "Russian Minority" in Ukraine: Regarding the Discussion at the Latest Session of the All-Union Central Executive Committee), *Tryzub* (Trident) 2, no. 30, May 9, 1926; reprinted in *Symon Petliura: Statti, lysty, dokumenty* (Symon Petliura: Articles, Letters, Documents) (New York: Ukrainian Academy of Arts and Sciences in the U.S., 1956), 378–383, esp. 383. Petliura started publishing his periodical *Tryzub*, named after the trident, or the heraldic coat of arms of the Ukrainian National Republic, when he settled in Paris in 1924.

37   Vlas Chubar (1891–1939), an ethnic Ukrainian, was chairman (from July 1923) of the Council of People's Commissars of the Ukrainian SSR and deputy chairman (from 1934) of the Council of People's Commissars of the USSR. He was arrested during the Great Terror in 1938 and executed in 1939.

38   Symon Petliura, "Lovtsi dush" (Soul Catchers), *Tryzub* 2, no. 26–27, April 18, 1926; reprinted in *Symon Petliura*, 364–374.

39   Case History LH47: Oleksandra Kostiuk (born March 14, 1899 near Kharkiv), in *Investigation of the Ukrainian Famine, 1932–1933: Oral History Project of the Commission on the Ukraine Famine*, edited by James E. Mace and Leonid Heretz (Washington, D.C.: U.S. Government Printing Office, 1990), vol. 1, 563.

dren; nevertheless, the demand for the Ukrainian-language publications grew. By 1927, approximately 88 percent of books were printed in Ukrainian, and the number of new periodicals reached 124 with 5 million in circulation.[40] New systematic studies and anthologies came out in print, including the history of the Ukrainian literature by Mykhailo Hrushevskyi, works by Serhii Yefremov, an anthology by Maxim Rylskyi, and textbooks with works of the Ukrainian literary classics.[41] Translations of foreign and national classical literature proliferated. Mykola Zerov [42] and Mykola Khvyliovyi [43] published a series of Ukrainian classical writers,

---

40   A. Karas, "Nacherk kulturnoho vidrodzhennia Ukraïny vid 1917 to 1933 rokiv" (An Essay on the Cultural Renaissance of Ukraine from 1917 to 1933), *Naukovyi zbirnyk UVU* (Scientific Publications of the Ukrainian Free University) (Munich, 1992), 228–229.

41   Movchan, "Na smertnii hrani," 17.

42   Mykola Zerov (1890–1937) was a poet, literary critic, leader of the Neoclassicists, a master of the sonnet form and a translator of ancient poetry. Documents about his life and work have been preserved in the Central State Archive Museum of Literature and Arts of Ukraine. Fund 28 consists of 15 case files covering the period from 1927 to 1935. Zerov maintained a prolific correspondence with his family and friends. His literary legacy is quite extensive. Some of the recent editions of Zerov's works and biographical literature include Serhii Bilokin, *Zakokhanyi u vrodu sliv: M. Zerov — dolia i knyhy* (In Love with the Beauty of Words: M. Zerov — Destiny and Books) (Kyïv: Chas, 1990); Marina Zerova, R. M. Korohodskyi, Mykhailyna Kotsiubynska, eds., *Nash suchasnyk Mykola Zerov: Zbirnyk statey* (Mykola Zerov, Our Contemporary: A Collection of Articles) (Lutsk: Teren, 2006); *Mykola Zerov. Vybrani tvory* (Mykola Zerov: Selected Works), compiled by Volodymyr Panchenko (Kyïv: Smoloskyp, 2015); and Volodymyr Panchenko, *Povist pro Mykolu Zerova* (The Story about Mykola Zerov) (Kyïv: Dukh i Litera, 2018).

43   Mykola Khvyliovyi (1893–1933) was a poet and writer. Born as Mykola Fitiliov to a family of teachers, Hryhorii Fitiliov and Elisaveta Tarasenko, in Trostianets, Kharkiv region, he dropped out of classical gymnasium to join Socialist Revolutionaries (SR). In 1915, he enlisted in the army. In 1917, during the February Revolution he headed the soldier's soviet in the Ukrainian Fourteenth Division, where he conducted educational and propaganda activities. After the October Revolution of 1917, his political leaning moved left. In 1918, he briefly served as chief of staff for SR T. Pushkar, who led an uprising against the Bolsheviks in the village of Murakhva, Bohodukhiv district (in 1933, this entire settlement was starved to death). In 1919, he joined the Communist Party. His famous novel, titled *Valdshnepy* (The Woodsnipes), described as "anti-party" and "counterrevolutionary," remained unfinished and unpublished when he committed suicide in May 1933. His last, and most radical work, "Ukraïna chy Malorosiia?" (Ukraine or Little Russia?), was suppressed by authorities. His vision of Ukraine's historic mission was known as Khvyliovism. His followers

among them Hryhorii Skovoroda, Ivan Kotliarevskyi, Taras Shevchenko, Petro Kulish, Ivan Nechui-Levytskyi, Panas Myrnyi, Olha Kobylianska, and Ivan Franko. In his introduction to selected works of Ivan Nechui-Levytskyi, Valerian Pidmohylnyi commented:

> The current time is characterized by a deep interest in the Ukrainian cultural heritage, primarily literature, where Ukraine's achievements are manifested in the most accessible form. What was accessible to a close circle of "nationally conscious Ukrainians" now becomes available for intellectual consumption by a large mass of Ukrainians. A new Ukrainian or a convert aspires to affirm oneself in being Ukrainian, to find a firm foundation after running in a rut on familiar tracks of the Russian culture. That is the reason why we publish the classics. I am curious if a new reader comes out of this gallery of our classicists like after a visit to a museum or a home full of life? Bored or excited?[44]

Not only literature, but Ukrainian theater flourished. After centuries of prohibition on using Ukrainian language on the stage, Russian theaters, including opera, were pushed out of Ukraine. Theaters that used to stage performances in Russian gave way to Ukrainian actors. In 1931, Ukraine featured 66 theaters that staged dramatic and musical performances in Ukrainian, 12 Jewish and 9 Russian theaters.[45] This was the time when Les Kurbas[46] experimented at his "Berezil" studio,[47] modernizing the Ukrainian national tradi-

---

were physically destroyed during the Stalinist terror or were forced to reconstruct themselves as socialist realists. His works were banned in the Soviet Union.

44   Valerian Pidmohylnyi, "Ivan Nechui-Levytskyi," in Ivan Nechui-Levytskyi, *Vybrani tvory* (Selected Works), vol. 1 (Kyïv: T-vo "Chas," 1927), vi.

45   Sheveliov, "Ukraïnizatsiia," 45.

46   Olga Bertelsen, *Les Kurbas i teatr "Berezil": Arkhivni dokumenty (1927–1988)* (Les Kurbas and "Berezil" Theater: Archival Documents, 1927–1988) (Kyïv: "Smoloskyp," 2016); Mayhill C. Fowler, *Beau Monde on Empire's Edge: State and Stage in Soviet Ukraine* (Toronto: University of Toronto Press, 2017).

47   Established in 1922, the theater moved from Kyïv to Kharkiv in 1926. The goal of the theater was to combine word, gesture, music, light, and decorative art, creating a live, thoughtful staging of classical and modern European as well as Ukrainian repertoire. See Y. Hirniak, "Berezil," in *Entsyklopediia Ukraïnoznavstva* (Encyclopedia of Ukrainian Studies), vol. II/1, edited by Volodymyr Kubijovyč (Paris–New York: Shevchenko Scientific Society and Molode Zhyttia Press, 1955), 114–115.

tion in theater arts. The Ukrainian cinema strengthened its repertoire. In 1928, thirty-six titles appeared on movie theater screens.[48]
By 1929, film studios were established in Odesa, Yalta, and Kyïv.

The nation reached out to its historical roots to recover its classical heritage. In 1928, the All-Ukrainian Ethnographic Society of
the All-Ukrainian Academy of Sciences organized expeditions to
excavate the mounds with treasures in Olbia and Chersonese[49] as
well as other ancient Greek cities on the sea coast in southern
Ukraine. A special ethnographic commission, established in 1920
and dismantled in 1933, collected and published fundamental studies and collections of Ukrainian folk songs. A museum of folk art in
Kyiv along with a museum of anthropology and ethnology named
after Fedir Vovk established a systematic study of the sources of the
Ukrainian folk tradition.[50]

Taken together these developments established the foundations of modern Ukrainian nation via creating its national narrative.
The Ukrainian idea became inseparable part of the collective consciousness. As Raïsa Movchan observed, "national art and literature were inherent in building a sovereign state in a spiritual, philosophical, and mental spheres."[51] During this fermenting of national consciousness, a "literary discussion" spilled over onto the
pages of Ukrainian periodicals.[52] The launching of this polemic
could be traced to the Russian Communist Party resolution, dated
June 18, 1925, that directed writers and poets to create proletarian
literature based on social class rather than national consciousness.

---

48 "Kino," in *Entsyklopediia Ukraïnoznavstva*, vol. II/3, edited by Volodymyr
    Kubijovyč (Paris–New York: Shevchenko Scientific Society and Molode Zhyttia
    Press, 1959), 1038.
49 Pontic Olbia, or simply Olbia, is an archeological site of an ancient Greek city
    on the shore of the Southern Bug estuary in the Mykolaiv region, whereas
    Chersonese (5th BC–14th AD) is an ancient Greek colony and outpost of the
    Roman and Byzantine Empires on the outskirts of Sevastopol, Crimea, in
    Ukraine.
50 Movchan, "Na smertnii hrani," 17.
51 Movchan, "Na smertnii hrani," 18.
52 For more about the literary discussion, see George S. N. Luckyj, *Literary Politics
    in the Soviet Ukraine, 1917–1934* (Durham and London: Duke University Press,
    1990); Myroslav Shkandrij, *The Ukrainian Literary Discussion of the 1920s*
    (Edmonton: Canadian Institute of Ukrainian Studies Press, 1992).

Consequently, during the peak of Ukrainization, from 1925 to 1928, this fateful "literary discussion" engulfed all of the intellectual circles. The main driving force behind the opposition to the ideological diktat was Mykola Khvyliovyi.[53] He inaugurated the polemic with a question: "Who is more vital to the Ukrainian literature: Zerov or Harkun-Zadunaiskyi[54]?" When the literary discussion turned political, Khvyliovyi went further, arguing for the need to reorient the Ukrainian literature toward "psychological Europe" in the direction "Away from Moscow!" in search of esthetic values beyond narrow class consciousness in order to create freely and overcome provincialism. Zerov also joined this discussion by calling upon writers to go back to the basics — Ad fontes! — the original sources of world and national literary traditions.[55]

Khvyliovyi's brave call to free Ukrainian literature from Russian influence caught Stalin's eye. It threatened the unity of the state that the dictator was building around the dominant Russian identity.[56] In his personal letter to Kaganovich, Stalin warned the Ukrainian communists about the "nationalist deviationism" and anti-Russian sentiments.[57] In 1928, the literary polemic was curtailed. Shumskyi's protest against Kaganovich's policy in Ukraine

---

53   For a detailed biography, see O. Han, *Trahediia Mykoly Khvyliovoho* (A Tragedy of Mykola Khvyliovyi) (Prague: Vyd-vo "Prometei," 1947). For a reappraisal of Khvyliovyi's fusion of political thought and literary craft, see Myroslav Shkandrij, "Mykola Khvyliovyi: u p'iatdesiati rokovyny smerti" (Mykola Khvyliovyi: In Memory of the 50th Anniversary of Death), *Suchasnist* (Modernity) 5 (1983): 7–14.

54   Vasylii Harkun-Zadunaiskyi is a character from Volodymyr Vynnychenko's story *Entrepreneur Harkun-Zadunaiskyi*, an embodiment of provincialism and *sharovarshchyna*.

55   Natalka Pozniak-Khomenko, "Spivets latyny i Ukraïny: do 130-richchia vid dnia narodzhennia Mykoly Zerova" (The Bard of Latin and Ukraine: In Memory of the 130th Anniversary of Mykola Zerov's Birth), *Ukrainian Institute of National Remembrance*, https://uinp.gov.ua/informaciyni-materialy/statti/spivec-latyny-y-ukrayiny-do-130-richchya-vid-dnya-narodzhennya-mykoly-zerova.

56   Malko, *The Ukrainian Intelligentsia and Genocide*, 72–73.

57   Josef Stalin, "Tov. Kaganovichu ta inshym chlenam PB TsK KP(b)U" (To Comrade Kaganovich and Other Members of the Politburo of the Central Committee of the Communist Party (Bolsheviks) of Ukraine), in *Mykola Khvyliovyi: Tvory v 5 tomakh* (Mykola Khvyliovyi: Collected Works), 5 vols., ed. Hryhorii Kostiuk (New York: "Smoloskyp," 1986), 485–489.

raised Stalin's ire.[58] Mykola Skrypnyk, who succeeded Shumskyi as Commissar of People's Education, was a staunch communist but no less a supporter of the Ukrainization policy. Skrypnyk committed suicide in 1933, two months after Khvyliovyi, whose death marked the end of Ukrainization.

Describing details of Skrypnyk's death, Royal Consul of Italy in Kharkiv Sergio Gradenigo in a confidential report to the Italian Embassy in Moscow, dated July 19, 1933, warned about genocidal capabilities of the Soviet regime: "The dying man was carried to the university clinic, where he regained consciousness during the blood transfusion. He told Postyshev, who had come by, that the real danger for Communism lay in Russian imperialism, which was on the rise." Consul Gradenigo concluded his report with a poignant observation that "the Ukrainian people are about to go into an eclipse, which could well turn out to be a night without end, because Russian imperialism, with its present tender mercies (i.e., tender Communist mercies), is capable of wiping a nation — nay, a civilization — right off the face of the earth if we aren't very careful."[59]

The rise of the OUN outside the borders of Ukraine and a growing anti-Soviet opposition inside the republic prompted the Kremlin to concoct a special operation to liquidate the so-called "underground counterrevolutionary organization," the Union for the Liberation of Ukraine (its Ukrainian acronym SVU). In spring and summer of 1929, the GPU arrested students and professors in Kyïv and other major cities on suspicion of plotting to overthrow the Soviet regime. In spring 1930, forty-five defendants were put on trial, over half of them academicians, professors, linguists, historians, and teachers of the Ukrainian language and history. Overall,

---

58 Shumskyi was dismissed from his post of Commissar of People's Education in 1927, arrested in 1933, sentenced to ten years of exile, and poisoned on Stalin's order in 1946 when he was returning by train to Ukraine.

59 Report by the Royal Consul Sergio Gradenigo from the Royal Consulate of Italy, Kharkiv, July 19, 1933-XI, Ref. No. 608/88 "Re: After the Suicide of Mykola Skrypnyk," in Commission on the Ukraine Famine, *Investigation of the Ukrainian Famine, 1932–1933: Report to Congress* (Washington, D.C.: U.S. Government Printing Office, 1988), 446–447.

the GPU arrested 30,000 innocent people accused of being associated with this organization.[60] As the GPU investigator formulated Moscow's intent: "We have to put the Ukrainian intelligentsia on its knees, this is our task—and it will be carried out; those whom we do not [put on their knees] we will shoot!"[61]

Stalin masterminded the SVU trial against the Ukrainian intelligentsia away from Kyiv, where most of the accused leaders were arrested, and used the stage in the Kharkiv Opera to add sinister theatricality to the trial. The GPU played a prominent role in both carrying out special operations to suppress uprisings in the countryside that engulfed over a million protesters against the Soviet regime with the help of the special GPU military units and pinning the blame on the elites most of whom previously served in various UNR government agencies between 1918 and 1922, before the noose of the USSR put an end on "separatist" urges. At the SVU trial the blueprint for extermination of Ukrainians was set in motion: independent farmers were the social base of the SVU, with the "headquarters" in the Ukrainian Academy of Sciences, supported by a network of "commanders" from the UAOC, and trained "militant terrorists" from the Union of the Ukrainian Youth (SUM). Cancerous growth of this process of eradicating Ukraine's intellectual and spiritual potential had gnawed at the body of the Ukrainian nation for decades.

The SVU trial foreshadowed Moscow trials of 1936–1938.[62] The SVU and the SUM were the first among fifteen major "under-

60   V. M. Nikolskyi, *Represyvna diialnist orhaniv derzhavnoï bezpeky SRSR v Ukraïni (kinets 1920-h – 1950-ti rr.). Istoryko-statystychne doslidzhennia. Monohrafiia.* (State Security of the USSR Repressions in Ukraine, late 1920s–1950s: A Historical-Statistical Study) (Donetsk: Vyd-vo DNU, 2003), 77–82.

61   Helii Sniehiriov, *Naboï dlia rozstrilu (Nenko moia, nenko . . .): liryko-publitsystychna rozvidka* (Bullets for Executions (Oh, Dear Mother...): A Lyrical-Journalistic Exploration) (Kyïv: Dnipro, 1990), 110; quoted in Yuri Shapoval, "The Case of the 'Union for the Liberation of Ukraine': A Prelude to the Holodomor?" *Holodomor Studies* 2, no. 2 (2010): 157–158; see also Anne Applebaum, *Red Famine: Stalin's War on Ukraine* (New York: Doubleday, 2017), 99.

62   George Liber, *Soviet Nationality Policy, Urban Growth, and Identity Change in the Ukrainian SSR, 1923–1934* (Cambridge: Cambridge University Press, 1992), 160–161.

ground counterrevolutionary organizations" the GPU "discovered" in Ukraine from 1930 to 1937.[63] The "discovery" of these organizations led to annihilation of pre-Soviet Ukrainian intelligentsia as a group.[64] Decades of scholarly accomplishments of the All-Ukrainian Academy of Sciences were wiped out, and research staff were purged.[65] The SVU trial and discovery of numerous "counterrevolutionary" groups marked the beginning of the end for Ukrainization.

According to Volodymyr Nikolskyi, during the early 1930s the largest number of arrests were among the intelligentsia (one third of the total), and 80 percent of them were Ukrainian.[66] Those who were not immediately executed, wasted their talents as slave labor in a network of prisons and camps.[67] As Lenin's right-hand man, Felix Dzerzhinsky was in charge of both agencies, state security and

63 For a list of the organizations, see Hryhory Kostiuk, *Stalinist Rule in the Ukraine: A Study of the Decade of Mass Terror (1929–1939)* (New York: Praeger, 1960), 85–86. The archives of the Security Service of Ukraine have a collection of 134 case files of fictitious organizations that were "foiled" between 1921 and 1934 by the watchful GPU sentinels of Soviet "law and order." These cases served as templates for future trials, with slight modifications based on the nature of the organization, but the methods of "uncovering" the enemies of the people remained repetitive. A sheer volume of these cases created an atmosphere of fear and suspicion in the society. In addition to "judges" that "protected" the public and the accused, mostly innocent silent victims forced to confess crimes they never committed, there were the onlookers in this theater of the absurd, the intimidated bystanders. See Nikolskyi, *Represyvna diialnist orhaniv derzhavnoï bezpeky SRSR v Ukraïni*, 62–67, 88.

64 Liber, *Soviet Nationality Policy*, 162–163.

65 A catalog of publications of the All-Ukrainian Academy of Sciences (founded in 1918, dissolved in 1929, and absorbed into the Academy of Sciences of the USSR) included 286 pages, listing 300 volumes of scientific studies, and 888 scientific publications compiled by 1,800 research associates. Six volumes of a Russian-Ukrainian dictionary, edited by linguist Serhii Yefremov, were removed from circulation. See Dmytro Solovey, *Golgota Ukraïny* (Drohobych: "Vidrodzhennia," 1993), 50–51. Academicians and research staff, who were purged, were stripped of their scientific titles and jobs, arrested, and prosecuted. See *TsDAVOU*, f. 166, op. 9, spr. 1459, ark. 18.

66 Nikolskyi, *Represyvna diialnist orhaniv derzhavnoï bezpeky SRSR v Ukraïni*, 49, 51, 89, 227, 230, 234–235, 313, 326, 330, 333, 339.

67 M. B. Smirnov, *Sistema ispravitelno-trudovykh lagerei v SSSR* (A System of Corrective-Labor Camps in the USSR), edited by N. G. Okhotin and A. B. Roginskii (Moscow: "Zvenia," 1998), http://old.memo.ru/history/nkvd/gulag.index.htm.

economic development. It was Dzerzhinsky's ingenious idea to set-
tle the devoid of intelligentsia places in the Russian wilderness to
explore and develop Russia's rich mineral resources with the sweat
and backbreaking forced labor supplied by the GPU in waves of
special operations against "counterrevolutionaries" and "sabo-
teurs."[68]

These "superfluous" members of the Ukrainian intelligentsia
became a slave labor force for industrial projects administered by
the GPU in desolate places scattered along the Arctic Circle. Only
three of the forty-five defendants in the SVU trial survived. Most
joined the groaning flotsam of humanity in concentration camps to
dig the Baltic Sea—White Sea Canal in the Far North or mine for
gold in Russian Klondike in Kolyma in the Far East. The Baltic
Sea—White Sea Canal project absorbed a wave of purges following
the order, telegraphed on December 14-15, 1932, to Russify all
Ukrainian institutions beyond the borders of the Ukrainian SSR and
before Pavel Postyshev's arrival to Ukraine on a special assignment
from Stalin. Postyshev came to destroy nationalism at the root,
which, at that time, was represented not just by Hrushevskyi and
Yefremov of the UNR, but by Ukrainian communists.[69]

New prisoners brought to GPU-run labor camps were Ukrainian farmers, participants in the uprisings of 1929-1932, teachers,
writers, poets, scholars, and even students.[70] These were not hard-
core incorrigible criminals, but political opponents of the regime
(sentenced for "counterrevolutionary crimes"), starving villagers

68   *TsOA KGB*, f. 2, op. 1, ed. kh. 1, l. 10–15; reprinted in *F. E. Dzerzhinsky—
rukovoditel VChK–OGPU: Sbornik dokumentov i materialov (1918–1926 gg.)* (F. E.
Dzerzhinsky—Leader of the VChK–OGPU: A Collection of Documents and
Materials, 1918–1926), eds. N. S. Zakharov, P. G. Grishin, and A. V. Prokopenko
(Moscow: Nauchno-izdatelskii otdel, 1967), 120–121. The collection of
documents has been preserved in the State Archives of the Security Service of
Ukraine *HDA SBU*, f. 13, od. zb. 603; quoted in Malko, *The Ukrainian
Intelligentsia and Genocide*, 91–92.
69   Semen Pidhainy, "Solowky Concentration Camp," in *The Black Deeds of the
Kremlin: A White Book*, vol. 1, *Book of Testimonies* (Toronto: Ukrainian Association
of Victims of Russian Communist Terror, 1953), 35. See also the original
Ukrainian language edition *Ukraïnska intelihentsiia na Solovkakh: spohady 1933–
1941* (The Ukrainian Intelligentsia on the Solovki: Memoirs, 1933–1941) (Neu
Ulm: Prometei, 1947), http://irbis-nbuv.gov.ua/ulib/item/ukr0000013314.
70   Pidhainy, "Solowky Concentration Camp," 36, 38.

who gathered stalks of wheat in the fields (charged with "theft of socialist property"), as well as members of the patriotic Ukrainian intelligentsia deemed "socially dangerous elements." They accounted for 52.8 percent combined for the three most frequently used articles of conviction as compared to only 7.5 percent convicted for "abuse of power, economic and military crimes" (Communist Party purges) during this period.[71]

In December 1934, four lists of banned authors were published, containing works by Ukrainian historians, sociologists, linguists, poets, writers, and anyone else who had been arrested. The authorities decreed that all their books must be removed from libraries, bookstores, and educational institutions. As scholars concluded, "the extermination of the intellectual class was accomplished by the extermination of their words and ideas."[72] In the Academy of Sciences of Ukraine, repressions swept 250 scholars, including 19 academicians. A terrible blow was dealt to Ukrainian literature: 89 writers were executed, 212 silenced, 64 exiled, and 83 forced to immigrate.[73]

Not only the Ukrainian literature was banned, but history was rewritten. According to the philologist Panteleimon Kovaliv, professor Hrushevskyi's account of Kyïvan Rus had been accepted in the USSR for fifteen years by historians A. Presniakov, M. Liubavskii, and even M. Pokrovskii. These scholars excluded the entire Kyïvan Rus period from the history of the Russian people. But three years after the Holodomor, a new theory of a "unified proto-Russian people" was added to history textbooks. After 1934, teachers who interpreted Shevchenko's "Haidamaky" as an example of the national liberation struggle could be fired, as was the case with a

---

71 Oleg V. Khlevniuk, *The History of the Gulag: From Collectivization to the Great Terror* (New Haven: Yale University Press, 2004), 323.

72 Bilokin, *Masovyi teror iak zasib derzhavnoho upravlinnia v SRSR*, vol. 2, 519–522; quoted in Applebaum, *Red Famine*, 220.

73 O. D. Boiko, Chapter 12.8. "Ukraïna i protses formuvannia totalitarnoho rezhymu v SRSR" (Ukraine and the Formation of a Totalitarian Regime in the USSR), in *Istoriia Ukraïny* (History of Ukraine), 7th ed. (Kyïv: Akademknyha, 2018), https://uahistory.co/pidruchniki/ukraine-history-boyko-7-edition-2018/69.php.

teacher in Artemivsk, Pastushko, who was denounced and dismissed as a "follower of the 'Ukrainian fascists' (!?) Hrushevskyi, Yefremov, and Hermaize."[74]

The situation for intellectuals from Ukraine became doubly hard in 1936–1937, when labor camp prisoners were deprived of even more "rights." More were thrown into isolation cells. "Fascist" trials were held more often and resulted in longer sentences. All those whose terms had expired were given an additional five to ten years. At the end of 1937, two long trains were convoyed out of the Solovetsky Islands. The first transport was made up of those who formed the major part of political prisoner-slaves, the Ukrainians.[75] They were among 1,111 from the Solovetsky camp executed on the eve of the twentieth anniversary of the October coup in 1937 — shot and buried at Sandarmokh, Karelian ASSR, Russia.[76] Among 289

74Y uri Mytsyk, "Chystky natsionalistiv u shkolakh 1934 r. (za materialamy kolyshnioho Dnipropetrovskoho oblasnoho partarkhivu)" (Nationalist Purges in Schools in 1934: Based on Materials from the Former Dnipropetrovsk Regional Party Archive), in *Ukraïnskyi holokost 1932–1933: Svidchennia tykh, khto vyzhyv* (The Ukrainian Holocaust 1932–1933: Testimonies of the Survivors), edited by Yuri Mytsyk (Kyïv: Vydavnychyi dim "Kyievo-Mohylianska akademiia," 2003–2013), vol. 3, 260. Hrushevskyi was exiled to Moscow in 1931 and died in 1934, in Kislovodsk, during a minor surgery; his body was returned to Ukraine in a casket. Professors Yefremov and Hermaize were exiled to the Solovetsky concentration camp. Serhii Yefremov, vice-president of the All-Ukrainian Academy of Sciences' governing council and secretary of its historical-philological division and the alleged leader of the fictional SVU, was sentenced to ten years of imprisonment and killed in 1939 in a labor camp. Yosyp Hermaize, secretary of the All-Ukrainian Academy of Sciences' historical division, after his release in 1934, was rearrested in 1937, and died in a labor camp after his sentence was extended by another ten years.

75 Pidhainy, "Solowky Concentration Camp," 40–41.

76 From August 11, 1937 to December 24, 1938, more than 9,000 victims of Soviet political repressions were executed by shooting and buried in three hundred separate burial trenches at Sandarmokh. These included 289 members of the Ukrainian intelligentsia. In 1997, "Memorial" Society located killing fields and burial sites at Sandarmokh near Medvezhiegorsk in Karelia (northwest Russia). Drawing on information from a KGB archive, Russian historian Yuri Dmitriev identified men and women shot at Sandarmokh as follows: 3,500 were inhabitants of Karelia, whereas 4,500 were prisoners working for the White Sea Canal, and 1,111 were brought there from the Solovky "special" prison. Alongside loggers and fishermen from nearby villages, farmers, writers and poets, artists, scientists and scholars, military leaders, doctors, teachers, engineers, clergy, and statesmen found their final resting place there. The position of the skeletons and other remains suggested that the prisoners had

Ukrainians were theater director Les Kurbas, writers Valerian Pidmohylnyi, Mykola Kulish, Mykola Zerov, and Krushelnytskyi with
his two sons.[77]

Similar to other cases of genocide, Ukrainian intelligentsia became the first target for liquidation. Their trials and tribulations
lasted from the 1920s through the 1930s, increasing in scope — until
all vestiges of Ukrainian aspirations to achieve sovereignty van-
ished. In the 1920s, deportations of ideological opponents did not
solve the problem. The solution came at the confluence of economic
necessity to build the first socialist state and the punitive use of political prisoners as slave laborers. As Leszek Kołakowski noted, the
Soviet variety of totalitarianism converted people into slaves, thus,
bearing certain marks of egalitarianism.[78]

The GPU special operation to liquidate "Ukrainian bourgeois
nationalism," which officially started in November 1932 under the
guise of a "grain procurement campaign," had been a decade in the
making. Those intellectuals who were candidates for deportation in
1922 were sitting on the court bench in 1929 as defendants in the
SVU trial. The old generation patriotic elites had to give way to Soviet cadres. In 1933, a process of crushing the backbone of Ukrainian society was accomplished by the genocidal famine — the Holodomor. It turned into an instrument of the nationality policy. On December 14, 1932, Stalin and Molotov signed a resolution of the Central Committee of the All-Union Communist Party (Bolsheviks) and

---

been stripped to their underwear, lined up next to a trench with hands and feet
tied, and shot in the back of the head with a pistol. See John Earl Haynes and
Harvey Klehr, *In Denial: Historians, Communism, and Espionage* (San Francisco:
Encounter Books, 2003), 117–118. For lists of names of prisoners executed at
Sandarmokh, see Yuri Dmitriev's *Mesto rasstrela Sandarmokh* (The Place of
Execution Sandarmokh) (Petrozavodsk, Russia, 1999) and *Mesto pamiati
Sandarmokh* (The Place of Memory Sandarmokh) (Petrozavodsk, Russia, 2019).
The current Russian leaders prosecuted Yuri Dmitriev on false charges and
imprisoned him for 13 years, later extending his term to 15 years.

77 For a list of the Ukrainian prisoners of the Solovetsky camp executed in 1937,
see Serhii Bilokin, "Rozstrilnyi spysok Solovkiv" (The Solovki's Killing List),
Literaturna Ukraïna (Literary Ukraine), no. 27 (4488), July 9, 1992, 8; see also
Bilokin, "Solovky," 283.

78 Leszek Kołakowski, "The Marxist Roots of Stalinism," in *The Great Lie: Classic
and Recent Appraisals of Ideology and Totalitarianism*, ed. F. Flagg Taylor IV
(Wilmington: Intercollegiate Studies Institute, 2011), 160.

the Council of Peoples Commissars of the USSR, which demanded "correct Ukrainization" in Soviet Ukraine and other regions densely populated by ethnic Ukrainians throughout the Soviet Union. The document also demanded a struggle against "Petliurists" and other "counterrevolutionary" elements, who this time were accused of organizing the famine.[79] This not only meant the end of "Ukrainization," but marked the decisive phase of the liquidation of the Ukraine-centered potential that was never supposed to revive.

The Stalinist regime used the famine and false stories about those who were responsible for it as a concrete pretext for mass-scale repressive campaigns, purges, and the like.[80] As a result of the purges, the rest of the Ukrainian intelligentsia became inert, intimidated by terror, unable to tell the truth about the Holodomor. Historians argue that the purges of the Ukrainian intelligentsia lasted until the dissolution of the Soviet Union in the 1990s.[81] Russification, imposed in 1938, was reversed only in 1989, when the Ukrainian language was proclaimed the state language of the republic, to lay the foundation for the declaration of state sovereignty and eventual independence of Ukraine in 1991, a reinstatement of independence first proclaimed in 1918 by the Ukrainian National Republic.

---

79   Yuri Shapoval, "Letters from Kharkiv: The Truth about the Holodomor through the Eyes of Italian Diplomats," *Den* (Day), November, 20, 2007; https://day.ky iv.ua/en/article/close/letters-kharkiv.

80   Shapoval, "Letters from Kharkiv."

81   Repressions against nationally conscious Ukrainians continued throughout the 1950s, when nationalist fighters from western Ukraine were exiled to concentration camps. The harassment of dissenters and human rights activists, among them Ukrainian poets, writers, and teachers charged with "anti-Soviet propaganda and agitation" lasted throughout Khrushchev's "Thaw" in the 1960s and the dissident movement of the 1970s, when the Ukrainian Helsinki Group was established, all the way to Gorbachev's perestroika. The last Ukrainian political prisoners were released from prison camps in 1991. Many died in exile. The survivors were rehabilitated in 1991. See Vasyl Ovsiienko, *Svitlo liudei: Spohady-narysy pro Vasylia Stusa, Yuria Lytvyna, Oksany Meshko* (People's Light: Memoirs-Essays about Vasyl Stus, Yuri Lytvyn, Oksana Meshko (Kyïv: URP, 1996) and Osyp Zinkewych, ed., *Ukraïnska Helsynska Hrupa, 1978–1982: Dokumenty i materialy* (The Ukrainian Helsinki Group, 1978–1982: Documents and Materials) (Toronto: V. Symonenko "Smoloskyp" Publishers, 1983). See also Olga Bertelsen, *In the Labyrinth of the KGB: Ukraine's Intelligentsia in the 1960s–1970s* (Lanham: Lexington Books, 2022).

From the Bolshevik coup in 1917 to the collapse of the Soviet Union in 1991, driven by the ideology of creating *Homo Sovieticus*, Soviet security police persecuted, tortured, and eventually exterminated from 20 to 60 million innocent victims.[82] Of those, the share of Ukrainians was 29.5 million.[83] On the ruins of the failed Soviet empire emerged the Baltic States and Ukraine to take up the cause to condemn the crimes of communism. The legal inheritor of the Soviet Union, the Russian Federation not only rehabilitated Stalinism, but brought back Leninism to occupied Ukrainian territories — all in the name of the new ideology of russkii mir (Russian World).[84]

Scholars have yet to agree on how to define the period from the 1920s to the 1930s: historians refer to it as the "cultural revolution," writers call it the "executed renaissance," and lawyers define it as Soviet genocide against Ukrainians.[85] Popularized by the

---

82 S. Courtois, "Zbrodnie komunizmu" (Crimes of Communism), in *Czarna księga komunizmu. Zbrodnie, terror, prześladowania* (The Black Book of Communism: Crimes, Terror, Persecution) by K. Bartosek, S. Courtois, J.-L. Margolin, A. Paczkowski, J.-L. Panné, N. Werth (Warsaw: Prószyński i S-ka, 1999). Rudolf Rummel wrote about 61,911,000 victims of the USSR in *Lethal Politics: Soviet Genocide and Mass Murder since 1917* (New Jersey: Transaction Publishers, 1990).

83 Oleksandr Hladun, "Viddaleni naslidky vtrat naselennya Ukraïny vid sotsialnykh katastrof u XX stolitti" (Distant Consequences of Population Losses in Ukraine from Social Catastrophes in the 20th century), in *Henotsyd Ukraïny u XX stolitti. Ukraïna pid okupatsiynymy rezhymamy: istorychni realii ta postkolonialnyi syndrom. Materialy tretioï Mizhnarodnoï naukovo-praktychnoï konferentsiï, Lviv, 4–5 kvitnya 2014* (Genocide in Ukraine in the 20th Century. Ukraine under Occupational Regimes: Historical Realities and Post-colonial Syndrome. Materials of the Third International Scientific and Practical Conference, Lviv, April 4–5, 2014), eds. L. Senyk, B. Morklianyk, R. Pak, M. Fitsuliak, I. Gavryliv, M. Chornopyskyi, I. Khoma, A. Fedoryshyn, O. Muzychko, O. Polyanskyi; All-Ukrainian Public Association "Society for the Revival of the Ukrainian Nation"; Lviv National University named after I. Franko; Lviv Polytechnic National University; Institute of Literary Studies of LNU named after I. Franko; KZ LOR "Lviv Historical Museum" (Lviv: Dobriy druk, 2015), 337–347.

84 Taras Kuzio, "Putin Forever: Ukraine Faces the Prospect of Endless Imperial Aggression," *Atlantic Council*, February 13, 2020, https://www.atlanticcouncil. org/blogs/ukrainealert/putin-forever-ukraine-faces-the-prospect-of-endless-i mperial-aggression/. Kuzio argues that Putin's mix of tsarist and Soviet Russian nationalism gave rise to a doctrine of *russkii mir*. The visible sign of it is the Russian World Foundation established in 2007.

85 Sheila Fitzpatrick, *Education and Social Mobility in the Soviet Union, 1921–1934* (Cambridge: Cambridge University Press, 1979), 116; Michael David-Fox, "What Is Cultural Revolution?" *The Russian Review* 58, no. 2 (1999): 181–201; Lavrinenko, *Rozstriliane vidrodzhennia*; Raphael Lemkin, "Soviet Genocide in the

writer and civic activist Ivan Drach, the term Holodomor—Soviet genocide against Ukrainians—has been carved into the depths of national memory.[86] The Ukrainian nonconformist intelligentsia, as guardians of the historical memory, preserved national traditions, refusing to serve the regime under heightened pressure to conform.[87] This stance echoes Václav Havel's ideas, expressed in his influential essay, "The Power of the Powerless," written in 1978, when the revisionist historians challenged the totalitarian paradigm. Havel advised his readers that the potential power in counteracting constant and total manipulation of society by the brutal and arbitrary regime lay in being unafraid to make a moral choice and to live as a responsible individual, "in truth."[88]

Dr. Victoria A. Malko is a faculty member and founding coordinator of the Holodomor Studies Program in the Department of History at California State University, Fresno. She is the author of *The Chechen Wars: Responses in Russia and the United States* (2015) and editor of *Women and the Holodomor-Genocide: Victims, Survivors, Perpetrators* (2019). She is the author of "Russian (Dis)Information Warfare vis-a-vis the Holodomor-Genocide" in a collective monograph *Russian Active Measures: Yesterday, Today, Tomorrow*, edited by Olga Bertelsen (2021). Her new monograph *The Ukrainian Intelligentsia and Genocide: The Struggle for History, Language, and Culture in the 1920s and 1930s* was published in 2021 by Lexington Books, an imprint of Rowman & Littlefield. She serves on the editorial board of *American History and Politics*.

Ukraine," (typewritten notes, folder 16, box 2, reel 3, ZL-273 "The Raphael Lemkin Papers, 1947–1959," Rare Books and Manuscripts Division New York Public Library), 1–8.

86 In Soviet Ukraine, Ivan Drach used the term "Holodomor" for the first time in his speech at a congress of the Ukrainian Writers Union. Olexii Musienko first used this term in his article, published in *Literaturna Ukraïna* (Literary Ukraine) on November 18, 1988. See James Mace, "Politychni prychyny holodomoru v Ukraïni (1932–1933 rr.)" (Political Causes of the Holodomor in Ukraine, 1932–1933), *Ukraïnskyi istorychnyi zhurnal* (Ukrainian Historical Journal) no. 1 (1995), 47.

87 Personal communication with Vira Annusova (b. 1956), a school teacher from the village Baranykivka, Bilovodsk district, Luhansk region, on November 20, 2019 in Kyïv, Ukraine.

88 Václav Havel, "The Power of the Powerless" (Essay), October 1978, 21. First published in the *International Journal of Politics* in 1979; available from the International Center on Nonviolent Conflict at https://www.nonviolent-conflict.org/resource/the-power-of-the-powerless/.

The Soviet Political Police in Ukraine

Polly Corrigan

The administration and management of the Soviet political police during the 1930s was a complex matter with different forces exerting multiple pressures on the institution at different points in time. These included the Soviet government, the leaders of the political police including Menzhinsky and Yezhov, the Soviet press, and the millions of Soviet citizens. As a result, the general picture of repression during this period was not a linear process rising to a terrible climax towards the end of the decade, but a more ad hoc situation that was often characterised by confusion and turmoil.

In this chapter, a focus on the activities and evolution of the Soviet political police in Ukraine during the 1930s offers a two-fold insight.

First, it will give the reader more detail about the running of local branches of the political police in Ukraine replicating this wider pattern of an institution in flux a great deal more than might be expected. The work of the Ukrainian political police came under sustained criticism from its own senior staff with questions asked about the working methods of agents and about the role of the management and other operational issues. Minutes of meetings demonstrate that it was not just operational matters that come under scrutiny but general questions on the fight against foreign spies, on the response to the Ukrainian famine and the relationship between the NKVD and other organs of the state. Taken together, these factors all indicate that the political police were not an institution with total control over every aspect of Soviet society but one that was characterised by doubts — and sometimes debate — on the part of the management and by change on the part of the staff. This change was not necessarily linear — a poorly functioning organisation remodeling itself into a more efficient organisation — but could be repetitive and counter-productive. While reforms were introduced, it is a matter of interpretation as to how successful they were.

Secondly, and as a result of this level of detail, this chapter will suggest that it is impossible to make generalisations about the repressions of the 1930s on an all-USSR basis; that the terror was experienced in different ways throughout the federation. It will go on to outline how decisions taken at national level were interpreted at local level and discuss the level of independence that individuals within the political police had to interpret these decisions in ways that suited them.

This chapter will begin with an analysis of the Ukrainian political police in the early part of the 1930s, looking at the particular challenges that the Ukrainian political police faced at this point. The chapter will then move chronologically through the decade, looking at primary evidence from the files of the SBU in Kiev to the Great Terror of the late 1930s and beyond.

Ukraine in the 1930s

In the early decades of the Soviet Union, there were particular characteristics that were unique to Ukraine and these influenced the direction that the repressions during the 1930s took. This may sound like a rather basic observation, but it is one that is worth taking a moment to consider. First, it was the largest of the non-Russian minorities that made up the Soviet Union. Secondly, it was a border nation, sitting between the Russian republic on one side and Poland on the other.[1] This combination resulted in a situation in which suspicion about Ukraine from those in Moscow grew quickly to quite serious levels, resulting in a very particular experience of the repressions of the 1930s which was arguably more acute than in other regions.

While the repression of the 1930s is often referred to as one homogenous event, the period can be divided up into many shorter phases and episodes. Similarly, due to the immense physical area of the Soviet Union, the terror was experienced differently in the various parts of the territory. The example of Ukraine is most instructive here. Ukraine had a unique experience of the 1920s and

---

1   Kuromiya, H, 'Report to Congress: Comission on the Ukrainian Famine (Book Review)', *Harvard Ukrainian Studies*, Vol 15 (1), 1991, p231.

early 1930s, and many of the issues that arose during this time would have echoes in the repression of the later 1930s.

In the early 1930s, the Ukrainian political police faced a number of challenges specific to the republic. First and foremost was the devastating famine and its aftermath. Another challenge was the perceived threat of Ukrainian nationalism.

The threat to Ukrainian nationalism resulted from the process known as Ukrainisation which had taken place during the 1920s. This policy had been controversial since the Bolsheviks first discussed it just after the October Revolution. The idea was to undermine potentially threatening nationalist movements within the many different republics and territories of the Soviet Union by allowing a certain amount nationalist activity. Terry Martin has described it as: '... a strategy aimed at disarming nationalism by granting what were called the "forms" of nationhood.'[2] Another scholar of the policy puts it more bluntly: in the case of Ukraine, the policy was put in place to 'win over' a hostile, mainly rural population.[3]

The policy got off to a shaky start in Ukraine, and it was not until Stalin sent Lazar Kaganovich to the republic in 1925 that things began to shift. Kaganovich oversaw the transformation of the party in Ukraine. All party documents began to be published in Ukrainian, party schools educated their pupils in Ukrainian and party members were ordered to study the language. Kaganovich met members of the Ukrainian intelligentsia and chatted to them in Ukrainian, and in 1927 addressed that year's party congress in Ukrainian too.[4] While Russian was still taught in all schools, Ukrainian became the language of public discourse, from street signs to books to film subtitles.[5] Ukrainian culture was also widely

2   Martin, T, *The Affirmative Action Empire: Nations and Nationalism in the Soviet Union*, Cornell University, 2001, p3.

3   Pauly, M, *Breaking the Tongue: Language, Education and Power in Soviet Ukraine, 1923-1934*, University of Toronto Press, 2014, p3.

4   Martin, T, *The Affirmative Action Empire: Nations and Nationalism in the Soviet Union*, Cornell University, 2001, p85.

5   Martin, T, p88.

supported, with party members taking classes in Ukrainian stud-ies.[6]

However, by the early 1930s this policy of placing Ukrainian language and culture at the centre of Ukrainian life—which had not been without its critics when it was first introduced—would be re-versed. Concessions to Ukrainian nationhood were now judged as too great a threat to the future of the Soviet state.[7] This measure would have far-reaching repercussions for many thousands of Ukrainian citizens. Cruelly, those who had been responsible for im-plementing party policy in the 1920s now became the target of those who had initiated the strategy. Teachers, academics, writers—all became the focus of the campaign against the dangerous 'national-ist deviation' and many were arrested.[8]

The implementation and reversal of the policy of Ukrainisa-tion had an impact on the course of political repressions in Ukraine in the 1930s in two sections of Ukrainian society. Although the So-viet intelligentsia generally found themselves often at the sharp end of investigations by the political police in the 1930s, the Ukrainian intelligentsia became synonymous with nationalism, something the Soviet authorities perceived as the most severe threat to its exist-ence in the region. Therefore, the persecution of the Ukrainian in-telligentsia became a particular feature of the Ukrainian terror.

Another section of society that suffered unimaginable adver-sity during this period was the Ukrainian peasantry. During the 1980s, the Ukrainian diaspora community in the United States be-gan to campaign for an investigation into the famine that took place in the 1930s. This sparked a raft of research from both Ukrainian historians and their counterparts abroad,[9] which established the

6   Martin, T, p90.
7   Yekelchyk, S, *Ukraine: Birth of a Modern Nation*, Oxford University Press, 2007, p114.
8   Yekelchyk, S, *Ukraine: Birth of a Modern Nation*, Oxford University Press, 2007, p114.
9   Kulchytskyi, S.V, 'Holodomor in the Ukraine 1932-1933: An Interpretation of the Facts', in Joack, Jannsen & Comerford (ed.s) *Holodomor and Gorta Mór: Histories, Memories and Representations of Famine in Ukraine and Ireland*, Anthem Press, 2014, p20.

main facts of the famine: during the latter part of 1932, and through-out 1933, millions of peasants died from a famine that resulted from problems with the grain harvest. While the famine occurred in other rural regions of the Soviet Union, Ukraine, exceptionally fertile as it was, suffered acutely during this famine, which followed quickly on the heels of the collectivisation of agriculture. What is also clear is that while the famine was ongoing, grain from the region of Ukraine was still being exported, leading some to see the famine as a man-made phenomenon.

This appalling and tragic chapter in Soviet history is probably one of the most contentious areas of Soviet history and still provokes serious debate both within the scholarly community and within Ukraine's contemporary political discourse. [10] Sensitive questions, such as whether the famine can be described as genocide are still being debated. Even the question of the number of people who died during the Ukrainian famine is not settled—with estimates ranging from 3-4 million up to around 10 million. A central thread of the debate focuses on what exactly Stalin's role was.[11] While these debates continue, what seems clear is that the famine changed the dynamics of the political repression that took place in Ukraine. While in many other areas of the Soviet Union, the bulk of the arrests took place in the second half of the decade, this was not so in Ukraine. In essence, the famine seems to have kicked off an early wave of arrests for political crimes, with nearly 75,000 people arrested by the political police in 1932, and nearly 125,000 arrested the following year. In the years 1934-1936, although arrests reached the tens of thousands, they were not as high as in these first two years.[12] These events shaped Ukraine during this period, and as we shall now see, they would also have a great impact on the Ukrainian political police over the coming decade.

---

10 See for example, Kasianov, H, 'Holodomor and the Politics of Memory in Ukraine After Independence' in Joack, Jannsen & Comerford (ed.s) *Holodomor and Gorta Mór: Histories, Memories and Representations of Famine in Ukraine and Ireland*, Anthem Press, 2014, pp167-188.

11 See for example, Kuromiya, H, 'Debate: The Famine of 1932-1933 Reconsidered', *Europe-Asia Studies*, Vol. 60, No. 4, June 2008, pp663-675.

12 Vasiliev, V, The Great Terror in the Ukraine, 1936-1938, in Ilic, M (ed), *Stalin's Terror Revisited*, Palgrave Macmillan, 2006, p141.

The Ukrainian political police in the early 1930s

In order to analyse the actions of the political police in Ukraine, it is useful to begin with an event that had significance for the political police throughout the Soviet Union. In July 1934, OGPU (Joint State Political directorate) was abolished and the NKVD assumed the functions of the political police. This USSR-wide, high-level, bureaucratic shift had structural, functional and legal implications for the political police.

An examination of documents from the files of the OGPU and the NKVD during 1934 confirms that the transformation of the political police was indeed taking place. Puzzlingly, however, this change did not coincide with the actual date of the transfer of duties from the OGPU to the NKVD. Reports from Vinnitsa (now known as Vinnytsia), a city to the southwest of the capital Kiev, show that change was already sweeping through the OGPU as early as January 1934. A first report on the work of agents written on 14 January 1934, nearly six months before the handover to the NKVD, explained that the department had spent the previous two months piloting measures to improve the work of agents in the city and throughout the surrounding regions.[13]

The report refers to the need to create 'concrete leadership', and discussed the process of identifying the most valuable agents in the division. It also contains a breakdown of the state of work by department, allowing a glimpse of the extent of the change that was taking place at this point. In the 1st Department, the work of the agents is described as having 'intensified' recently, the most valuable agents in the department having been selected and encouraged to communicate more effectively with the operatives 'in order to raise the quality of... work'. To further aid the department, all agent work was now carried out according to a planned calendar.[14]

The report goes on to detail some of the work of the most valuable agents, including an unlikely candidate named as Agent

---

13   Archives of the *Slyzhba bezpeki Ukraini* (Security service of Ukraine) hereafter SBU, F.16, Op.01, Spr30
14   SBU, F.16, Op.01, Spr.15, p.33

Brovar. Despite having spent 10 years in a camp for counter-revolutionary activity, Brovar's new duties involved reporting on 'the mood of Ukrainian chauvinist elements' at his place of work, the Vinnitsa State Typography. Interestingly, he also worked by night as a proofreader for 'Bolshevist Pravda'. Another of Brovar's colleagues, Agent Vateran, had a background as a chemical engineer and also worked as a border guard; however, his work for OGPU was to shed light on those who seek to steal technical intelligence.[15]

The report also gives details of the changes happening within the 2nd, 3rd and 4th Departments. It is apparent that some 16 members of the network of informers had been purged from the 2nd Department.[16] Both the 2nd and 3rd Departments had made commitments to better internal communication. Furthermore, the 2nd and 3rd Departments were both determined to offer assistance to the Regional Apparatus (*Raiapparat*) of the GPU (State Political Directorate); the 2nd Department in assisting with the recruitment of new agents[17] while the 3rd Department was making a study of all the valuable agents of the Regional Apparatus.[18]

Although this report from January 1934 is over 20 pages long and contains much detail on the work of the Vinnitsa OGPU, it was followed up by a second report written in April 1934 on the restructuring of work of special agents from the same division. This report, which is more strongly worded and addressed to the Chairman of the Ukrainian political police, is a response to a directive from Ukrainian State Political Directorate (GPU) and the OGPU Special Department. It lists 'very serious defects' identified in the work of the political police in this region under five broad headings including: use of under-qualified operatives, lack of discipline and initiative, a divide between the most qualified operatives and the rest of the staff, and even 'failures in appearance'. Problems in management are also identified, including another reference to the failure to provide 'concrete leadership'.[19]

---

15   SBU, F.16, Op.01, Spr.15, p.34
16   SBU, F.16, Op.01, Spr.15, p.37
17   SBU, F.16, Op.01, Spr.15, p.43
18   SBU, F.16, Op.01, Spr.15, p.47
19   SBU, F.16, Op.01, Spr.15, p.21-22

This list was followed by a catalogue of measures that the report states will constitute a 'radical restructuring of the work of agents'. There was a heavy emphasis on changes of practice within the leadership of the division including a commitment to the management working much more closely with operatives, and taking responsibility for the most 'serious' part of the work done by the division. As for changes in the work of the agents themselves, there were plans for them to submit daily reports about their activities.[20] The report closed with another list of commitments to 'consolidate' the changes already made, including recruiting new agents, promoting those who are deemed most promising and the screening of all agents.[21]

Contrast these reports from Vinnitsa in early in 1934 with a set of reports that were made in August that year after the transfer to the NKVD had been made. These files make regular reference to the changes that were taking place within the political police at this time. However, they also give an insight into more general issues and challenges that the Ukrainian NKVD's senior staff were wrestling with at that point. The files were the result of a series of meetings held throughout August 1934. Vsevelod Balitsky, then head of the NKVD in Ukraine, was present at all these meetings, along with a couple of other senior staff members. Most of the meetings were held on consecutive days in August, suggesting that the NKVD leadership in Ukraine perceived a compelling need for a wide-ranging survey into the affairs of the political police at this point.

Balitsky was the son of an accountant, and had been a member of the communist party since 1915. He had worked in the political police since 1918, working for most of that time in Ukraine, and had risen to the position of OGPU Plenipotentiary by the summer of 1934. On the 15th of August, he took up a new post as the head of the Ukrainian NKVD, a position that he would remain in until May of 1937.[22] Balitsky's new role in the NKVD illustrates that the change from OGPU to NKVD did not necessarily signify a clean

20   SBU, F.16, Op. 01, Spr.15, p.21-22
21   SBU, F.16, Op. 01, Spr.15, p.28
22   Petrov, N & Skorkin, K, *Spravochnik*, http://www.memo.ru/history/NKVD/
      kto/biogr/gb31.htm

slate; plenty of staff that had worked for the OGPU continued to work in similar roles in the NKVD.

Balitsky was clearly keen to make changes — and to be seen to be making changes. He attended his first meeting about the future of the NKVD on 7 August 1934 before he had technically taken up his new role within the organisation. Minutes from this meeting, headed 'Meeting at the Narkom [People's Commissariat] for Internal Affairs USSR [23] on the questions of the construction of the NKVD', indicate that at this point a great deal of building work was taking place, with at least three new buildings in the pipeline for the Ukrainian NKVD by 1935, with a budget of 13m rubles being spent on building work in that year alone in Kyiv.[24]

Once Balitsky had planned out the necessary building work to facilitate the work of his staff, he began to assess exactly how well the NKVD was functioning and to identify areas of weakness and how to address them. On 22 August, he had a meeting with the Odessa Oblast Administration followed by a further meeting on 27th August, this time of the Kiev Oblast Administration, to discuss 'questions on the work of the Kiev Oblast Administration of the NKVD'.[25] Again, there was a slight change of tone and of emphasis in this report, outlining changes that had been made within the political police during the year, but also discussing the work that they had carried out, and examining the broader issues and challenges of the year. The format of the report is a series of statements from various members of staff, and the tone is set by the first testimony from an agent simply referred to as Comrade Rozanov, probably Alexander Borisovich Rozanov, a member of the NKVD since 1918 and head of the Kiev Oblast OGPU until 10 July 1934 before being renamed as the new head of the Kiev Oblast NKVD after a five day hiatus.[26]

---

23   In this case, USSR stands for Ukrainian Soviet Socialist Republic, rather than the Union of Soviet Socialist Republics (in Russian: YCCP).

24   SBU, F.16, Op. 01, Spr.15, p.9

25   SBU, F.16, Op. 01, Spr. 13, p.20

26   Petrov, N & Skorkin, K, Spravochnik: http://www.memo.ru/history/NKVD/kto/biogr/gb422.htm

Rozanov gave a quick survey of the work of the OGPU/NKVD in 1934 kicking off with 'a number of major cases', before the attention of the political police switched to carrying out a major purge against counter-revolutionary elements in the city of Kiev. During this purge, some 25,000 people were exiled from Kiev, with a further 18,000 removed to beyond the 50-kilometre zone.[27]

Rozanov then reported on the changeover from the OGPU to the NKVD involving 'a period of immediate reform of the work of agents... Orders from Com. [rade] YAGODA and Com. BALITSKY were studied at... meetings...' The orders from Yagoda (then head of the NKVD) and Balitsky inevitably brought change, including a review of the agents working in the regions, starting to try and resolve issues with the management of agents, and a number of other 'immediate changes', including the use of agents working undercover.[28]

In a clear demonstration of how the specific events of Ukraine influenced the policy and practice of the political police, Rozanov then moves on to quite a different subject: that of the famine that had taken place in Ukraine during the previous years. As he introduces the topic, Rozanov's tone seems to change a little; indeed he appears to delay a little before coming to his central point. He begins by introducing the topic, saying: 'I want to dwell on issues related to the village.' Then he comes to the point: 'As we all know, the year 1933... was very severe and we had mass cases of famine [goloda].' Rozanov continues for a couple more sentences on the broader picture — discussing the harvest and the numbers of beetroot that were planted in 1934 — before coming to the question specifically connected with the activities of the political police. Once again, his tone almost seems hesitant as he makes his point: 'I want to particularly touch on one question, connected with the village.' Finally, he comes to the point: 'This question of mass exclusions from the collective farms. Lately we have noted mass exclusions from collective farms for violation of internal regulations, and very

---

27   SBU F.16, Op. 01, Spr. 13, p.20
28   SBU F.16, Op. 01, Spr. 13, p.20

often they exclude poor people, who did not work badly on the collective farm. This year 30,000 people were excluded from collective farms in Kiev Oblast. I believe that this phenomenon should be considered [*zadumat'siya*].'[29]

The tone is muted (and the last word a little ambiguous in translation) but the shift is clear. Rozanov is calling for an end to the policies enacted against Ukraine's rural population, and the fact that he has to do so in such a low-key language only serves to illustrate what a sensitive topic this remains. However, Rozanov has one more point to add on this question, and seems to suggest that the situation is not yet fully resolved: 'I want to note... increased counter-revolutionary activity of the clergy in the village. This greatly complicates our work in the village.'[30] Is this comment a genuine observation about the clergy? Or is it a way to leave the door open for possible future reprisals against the rural population? It is hard to say, but it strikes a jarring note after the relatively conciliatory statement that directly precedes it.

The meeting then proceeded with statements from other members of the staff. Comrade Alexandrovsky comments that there have been 'significant shifts' in the work of the Kiev Oblast Special Department. He went on to express his concerns that although 'considerable work' has been done on searching for German spies on Soviet territory he has fears about spies from other nations, specifically Poland: 'I want to emphasize that Polish work is given insufficient attention.' He goes on to suggest his remedy for the situation: 'I think the Kiev Regional Administration [*Oblupravenniyu*] more than any other need to look for a link between the Germans and the Polish, about which Com.[rade] Balitsky spoke at the last meeting.'[31]

Comrade Krivets, who was also present at the Odessa meeting, had an eventful 1934. He began the year as the Deputy Head of the Dnepropetrovsk OGPU. From March to July 1934, he had taken

29   SBU F.16, Op. 01, Spr. 13, p.21
30   SBU F.16, Op. 01, Spr. 13, p.21
31   SBU F.16, Op. 01, Spr. 13, p.22

up a post as Deputy Head of the Economic Management subdivision of the OGPU (tasked with fighting economic counter-revolutionary activity including sabotage, economic espionage, abuse of power and bribery). With switchover, Krivets took on the very same role but now as *head* of the Economic Department of the NKVD.[32]

At this meeting, Krivets had stuck to his economic brief, making some minor points about industry in Kiev ('Industry in Kiev is small ...') and then going on to mention the provision of food, saying: 'About bread – there is not enough information about the fight against speculators in both city and village.' This remark, the only other time that the food situation is mentioned during this meeting, is both short and direct – a contrast to the earlier remarks made by Rozanov.

Krivets also registers his concerns about methods of working within the institution itself, specifically problems of: 'inconsiderate attitude towards valuable agents'. He ended with an ominous observation: 'With this attitude, the agency will not work.'[33]

Two further comrades, Bukshpan and Katsnelson, also raise points about general administrative problems within the NKVD. Bukshpan reported problems in the relationship between the NKVD and the Procurator, stating: 'I want to draw the attention of Com. Rozanov, that recently there is a number of conflicts with the Procurator Com. Shriftov, who is behaving wrongly. The Regional Admin does not inform com. Rozanov about all these conflicts, due to which there is no proper response to the behavior of the Procurator.'[34]

In summary, 1934 was a year of great change for the Soviet political police. The reports from the first half of the year confirm that those within the political police are aware of major problems within the organisation, both on the part of agents and managers. These reports are something of a puzzle. Written well before the OGPU was abolished, they nevertheless suggest new measures to

---

32   Petrov, N & Skorkin, K, *Spravochnik*: http://www.memo.ru/history/NKVD/
        kto/biogr/gb255.htm
33   SBU F.16, Op. 01, Spr. 13, p.23
34   SBU F.16, Op. 01, Spr. 13, p.24

be implemented a few months before the transfer from OGPU to NKVD is to take place. It could be interpreted that these changes were made in anticipation of the more substantial changes that would inevitably accompany a major reorganisation. However, the documents make no reference to the coming reorganization. So it's possible that, these changes were made without the knowledge of plans for change in the future and therefore a futile, even wasteful exercise soon be superseded by a new wave of intensive change.

The Ukrainian NKVD in the later 1930s

The upheaval that took place within the NKVD during the early 1930s continued into the second half of the decade, the time of the Great Terror—with a wider context that by the end of the 1930s, it was not just the political police that had suffered violent transformation. Many of Ukraine's political institutions by this point were engulfed in a similar level of chaos.

The onset of this political turbulence in Ukraine seems to date from the summer of 1936 when the trial of old Bolsheviks Zinoviev and Kamenev in Moscow prompted the arrest of a handful of party bureaucrats. But it was not until the new year that any real changes began. In January 1937, a decree issued by the Soviet leadership in Moscow signalled what was to come—it was titled 'On the unsatisfactory Party leadership of the Kiev *obkom* and deficiencies in the work of the Ukrainian Central Committee'. Days later, Kaganovich arrived in Kiev to begin the process of replacing most of the Ukrainian party leadership including the head of the Kiev *obkom* and most of the Ukrainian Central Committee.[35] These major changes echoed over the coming months with similar purges of the Ukrainian Sovnarkom and other departments, as well as newspapers and radio stations.

Whether by accident or design, these purges rendered Ukrainian government almost impossible by the beginning of 1938 as so many individuals had been purged: 'By the beginning of 1938, the

---

35   Vasiliev, V, 'The Great Terror in the Ukraine, 1936-1938', in Ilic, M (ed), *Stalin's Terror Revisited*, Palgrave Macmillan, 2006, p142.

Ukrainian Politburo, Central Committee and Sovnarkom had practically ceased to exist as a result of the repressions. The republican People's Commissariats were unable to function normally.'[36]

It was of course Nikita Khrushchev was sent by Stalin to restore order as he recalls in his memoirs: 'In 1938 Stalin called me in and said: "We want to send you to Ukraine, so that you can head up the party organisation there. Kosior is being transferred to Moscow to be Molotov's first deputy chairman of the Council of People's Commissars…'[37] Khrushchev recalls expressing doubts about his own suitability for the post but went nevertheless, and by the summer of 1938 the Ukrainian Politburo and Central Committee were once again operational.

Against this background, the operations of the NKVD during the period do not appear to be quite as contradictory as they did in the earlier years of the 1930s. In fact they fit a very similar pattern. However, at the centre of the Ukrainian NKVD, greater change was underway. Balitsky, who had been chief of the NKVD in Ukraine since its inception, was dismissed on 11 May 1937. His replacement did not take up his post until 14 June 1937, leaving the whole Ukrainian organisation without a leader for over a month. When he finally arrived, the new leader, I.M. Leplevsky, only lasted in the position for a mere seven months, before he too was replaced. This time the handover was immediate with A.I. Uspensky, previously head of the NKVD in the Orenburg oblast,Uspensky taking up his position on the very day that Leplevsky left.[38]

The level of chaos within the NKVD during this period is further underscored by the intervention of the central head of the organisation, Nikolai Yezhov. It has been argued that the Ukrainian NKVD during the great terror worked fairly independently.[39] However, Yezhov made regular appearances whether in person or via

36   Vasiliev, V, 'The Great Terror in the Ukraine, 1936-1938', in Ilic, M (ed), *Stalin's Terror Revisited*, Palgrave Macmillan, 2006, p143.

37   Khrushchev, S, (ed.), *Memoirs of Nikita Khrushchev – Vol 1: Commissar, 1918-1945*, Pennsylvania State University Press, 2004,

38   Petrov & Skorkin, *Kto rukovodil NKVD 1934-1941: Spravochnik*, Moskva, 1999, accessed online: http://old.memo.ru/history/nkvd/kto/index.htm

39   Vasiliev, V, The Great Terror in the Ukraine, 1936-1938, in Ilic, M (ed), *Stalin's Terror Revisited*, Palgrave Macmillan, 2006, p148.

the various documents by and through which the terror was formally detailed.

Yezhov initially approved the Ukrainian NKVD's estimates of how many people were to be executed and how many were to be exiled. Throughout the autumn and winter of 1937, Yezhov and Leplevsky were in regular contact over the increases in the number of people to be purged. But then in early 1938, after well over 150,000 arrests had been made in Ukraine, Yezhov decided that the work of the Leplevsky was too 'rough and clumsy' and he was edged out in favour of the had of the NKVD in the Orenburg oblast, A Uspensky.[40]

This was not the only change that would have significance for the Ukrainian NKVD around this time. In the same period, Khrushchev was appointed first secretary in Ukraine and in February of 1938, Yezhov himself arrived in Kiev to oversee Uspensky's activities, and to initiate a new wave of arrests, announcing that a further 30,000 people were to be executed.[41]

What evidence do we have that change was taking place throughout the NKVD in Ukraine during these years? It seems that structurally, the organisation underwent considerable change during this period, as historians Zolotarov and Stepkin have suggested: '[In]… 1937-1938 the organizational structure of the NKVD, in the centre, and in the field is constantly changing…'[42]

This is not unexpected, as change was a feature of the organisation of the central Soviet-wide NKVD throughout the later 1930s. In fact, the operational divisions of the whole of the NKVD were reorganised twice in 1938, first in March and then later in September. In the March reorganisation, four new divisions were added to the existing twelve. The first new division was responsible for monitoring military organisations as well as the police, fire brigade and the offices where new army recruits would enlist. The second was the department for defense industry, the third a general department for industry and the fourth a department to oversee trade and

---

40 Vasiliev, V, 2006, p149-150.
41 Vasiliev, V, 2006, p150.
42 Zolotarev, V, Stepkin,V, *ChK-GPU-NKVD v Donbasse : Liudi i dokumenty 1919-1941*, Donetsk, 2010, p33.

agriculture. These changes might seem to be explained by the necessity to prepare for war. However the reorganisation also saw responsibility for special operations shift from the Fifth Division of the GUGB (counter-intelligence) NKVD to the 2nd Department of the NKVD, and the responsibility for six other divisions shift from the GUGB NKVD to the NKVD — including Transport and Communications, the Foreign Department, Accounting and Registration, the Special Department in charge of encryption, and the Prison department. A mere six months later, another major reorganisation took place in which responsiblility for very major department was once again switched.

While a reorganisation taking place in September might seem just about plausible — as this was the time when the purges were starting to wind down, and two months before Yezhov had been removed from his position as head of the NKVD, the earlier reorganisation in the spring of 1938 took place while the Great Terror was still in full swing. The very fact that two reorganisations took place in the same year suggests a high degree of internal upheaval, possibly the result of operatives attempting to become familiar with a new field of work at high speed.

This level of change was not replicated throughout the Soviet Union. In the Donetsk NKVD, the structure of the political police remained more or less unchanged from January 1937 until June 1938 during which time it was divided into twelve departments — with the 6th Department (Transport) disbanded in August 1937, after the creation of a centralized Rail-Transport Department of the Ukrainian NKVD which bypassed the local offices entirely.[43]

At first glance, this change might not seem so important. After all, it's only the transport department — and therefore not closely associated with the delicate work of security operatives such as Special Operations or the Secret Political Department. On closer inspection, however, it becomes clear that this centralised transport department was far more significant than its name suggests. It seems that the *de facto* operations of this department encompassed

43   Zolotarev, V, Stepkin,V, *ChK-GPU-NKVD v Donbasse : Liudi i dokumenty 1919-1941*, Donetsk, 2010, p33-34.

a far broader sphere than simply transport, being responsible for some of the most important aspects of security at this point, including counter-intelligence and had the power to arrest and try their suspects as Zolotarev and Stepkin make clear in their investigation of the Donetsk NKVD: ' GUGB NKVD was essentially the department of operative-territorial security, having in its composition operative, counter-intelligence, secret-political and special departments, and independently conducting arrests, investigations and execution.'[44]

In this situation, we see an even greater level of confusion. After all, the NKVD had been divided into 12 departments for a number of reasons: to spread responsibility evenly; to allow its workers to specialise in one field; and to avoid any single department becoming overly powerful. The fact that in reality, the Rail Transport Department held such power, authorised in August 1937 just as the Great Terror got underway, suggests a recognition somewhere of a need for an almost informal structure to continue the work that needed to be done. The fact that this department was centralised and able to bypass local bureaucracy seems to suggest a desperate desire to be able to act without scrutiny. The fact that it was created in August 1937s suggests a system where decisions were made very quickly, perhaps even spontaneously. This was not an organisation in which the terror was planned meticulously months or even years ahead. It was an organisation where expediency, tempered with fear, was the key motivation for staff — and, unsurprisingly, this led to chaos throughout the NKVD during this time.

In all of the evidence that is available about the NKVD in Ukraine during the 1930s, there is, in fact, only one area in which logic and order reign: the files that were kept of the investigations and interrogations that took place during these years. In these files, everything is orderly, meticulous and tidy, the records progressing from one point to the next with clarity and precision in complete contrast to the swirling incoherence that characterised the real world of the NKVD. There are many examples of this ordered tone

---

44   Zolotarev, V, Stepkin,V, *ChK-GPU-NKVD v Donbasse : Liudi i dokumenty 1919-1941*, Donetsk, 2010, p35.

and approach in the reports complied in the summer of 1937 – only weeks before the Great Terror was formally launched with the NKVD's order number 00447 at the end of July and, following the arrest of Marshal Tukhachevsky and five other prominent Soviet military leaders, the start of a massive purge of the Soviet army.

From the records of the Donetsk regional NKVD emerges the case of Frolov (no first name given) who was under investigation for being a member of various counter-revolutionary groups. He admitted that he first became a member of such a group in 1929 while at the Red Army Infantry School in Vladikavkaz, becoming involved in a 'right-wing counter-revolutionary group' as well as denouncing the policies of collectivisation and industrialisation in a meeting. A few years later, in Odessa, Frolov was associated with a counter-revolutionary group based in another educational establishment. This time the group was made up largely of Trotskyites, and had been carrying out 'active Trotskyite work' among the students of the college. Frolov had given the names of those with whom he colluded in Odessa, and they include the school director, a man named Feldman, another academic, Professor Maleev, a professor of the history of the trade unions,) and Professor Petrov, a professor of the history of Leninism. Finally, in 1937, Frolov was found to be part of yet another counter-revolutionary organisation is Kramatorsk. The investigation was continuing, with a stated priority to identify other members of this organisation.[45]

Many of the other cases in the file follow the same pattern. A suspect is identified or comes forward to identify himself (and most of those under investigation in this particular file are male). He admits membership of a counter-revolutionary group, and goes on to name a small group of co-conspirators. Most of those named, if not all, are usually identified as Trotskyites. However, one case in this file, under investigation by the Dnepropetrovsk NKVD, stands out as slightly different. This is the case of Andrei Yakovlevich Budny, the 2nd Secretary of the Zaporozhye Gorkom.

---

45   SBU, F.16, Op.1, Spr. 109, p51-52.

While Budny's crime was similar to the rest, his testimony was notable because of the very different calibre of people that he denounced. Instead of the circle of conspirators centring around one local institution, Budny accused people far beyond—and above— his local sphere, and seemingly unconnected to his personal or professional life. They were in fact a rather impressive bunch: Mikhailov, the current head of construction of the Palace of the Soviets in Moscow; Grando, his deputy; and another man who was head of an aviation factory. Later on in his testimony, Budny also names one Schifman, someone apparently working on the construction of the Palace of the Soviets along with two students. Later in his testimony, Budny adds the names of a handful of people based more locally in Dnepropetrovsk. Interestingly, the link between Budny and the first group of counter-revolutionaries that he has named is not made clear. There is nothing in Budny's evidence to suggest a link, nor is any explanation offered by any of the officers working on the case.

Conclusion

The NKVD in Ukraine during the 1930s was an organisation that was subject to a high level of bureaucratic turbulence that took many forms. It underwent reform and was subjected to high levels of criticism from within its own ranks for a wide range of operational failings. It suffered interference from its political masters and from its own central leadership in Moscow. As the Great Terror got underway, it proved itself to be a highly effective organisation, arresting thousands of people in the space of a few months. This took place against a background of turmoil within the organisation including meaningful intervention from Yezhov that included the removal of the head of the Ukrainian NKVD as well as reorganisation of the various departments of the NKVD itself and the formulation of ad hoc arrangements to make sure that the arrests that were deemed necessary actually happened.

Yet when we turn to the documentary records of the period, all is calm and measured. Meetings are painstakingly minuted, despite the criticisms contained therein. Testimonies of suspects, arrested en masse and at great speed, are detailed, and, in a fashion, make sense. While we may be skeptical about the truth of their strikingly similar confessions, the testimonies have their own narrative structure that hang together reasonably well. While the *subject* of the documents may be the shortcomings of the NKVD itself or the perceived threats to the Soviet Union in the form of counter-revolutionaries and Trotskyites, the *manner* of their documentation does not speak of panic or chaos. The pages themselves are neat and tidy, either type-written or in fine copperplate handwriting. Occasionally, a sentence or paragraph has been crossed through with a pencil, or highlighted with a rippling line in the margin. There are sometimes a few words written in the margin. But these do not appear to contradict or reinterpret the substance of these documents. What is written here is a solid, stable of the work of the NKVD, that might have been reassuring for those who wrote it.

In order to get a better understanding of this internal world of the interrogation file, it is useful to examine a sample in more detail. In the next chapter, the interrogation files of several Ukrainian writers are scrutinized. One advantage of the files of writers is that while they largely follow the pattern of other interrogation files, they are generally more detailed. A consideration of why this was the case will be explored, along with a detailed analysis of exactly what was unique about the interrogations of Ukrainian writers.

Ukrainian Writers and the Dynamics of Security Services

Polly Corrigan

In the last chapter, it became clear that the Soviet political police in Ukraine was an institution with a peculiar internal dynamic. While the Ukrainian political police were extremely active in their work, arresting and executing many thousands of suspects during the 1930s, they were also under considerable pressure from both internal and external sources to improve their work, due to perceived failings. This led to a high level of upheaval within the organisation. Yet, despite all this upheaval and chaos, the work of arresting suspects went ahead, accompanied by the meticulous record keeping of the NKVD, most notably in the form of the files that were kept of interrogations of suspects. Katerina Clark sums up this paradox neatly:

> 'Western historiography has tended to foreground the arbitrariness of the purges and the insubstantiality, not to say fantastic nature, of the charges leveled, yet generally for each purge victim care was taken to provide a written record of the interrogation justifying the verdict.' – K. Clark, *Moscow – The Fourth Rome*, p93.

In this chapter, we will examine in close detail the interrogation file and will attempt to get to the heart of Clark's observation. While NKVD operatives at all levels understood the necessity for process to be observed, the fact was that the purges were driven by results with the limits set in advance—reflecting the great struggle between Soviet legality and pragmatism in the mid-1930s.

The leaders of the USSR in the 1930s were not unique here. Many leaders find that the laws and practices of their countries can act as a brake for the policies that they wish to implement. Samantha Power, a recent US ambassador to the United Nations, gave an interview to the *New Yorker* in which she commented that 'as time wears on, I find myself gravitating more and more to the G.S.D. [Get-Shit-Done] people.'[1]

The Soviet interrogation file is the physical embodiment of the need of the Soviet leadership to 'get shit done', and yet still observe the legal requirements.

Interrogation files in context

The Soviet Union was late to develop a system of national archives. The French had set up their *Archives Nationales* in 1790, and the rest of Europe had followed suit soon afterwards. This development was itself rooted in the European nineteenth century historical thought, and specifically in the belief that the use of historical archives would enable future historians to render the past as it really was through the 'scientific' presentation of the 'facts' bestowed with authority by their place in the archive.[2] Meanwhile Russia under the Tsars had no system of archives at any point.

Therefore when, in June 1918, Lenin signed a decree ordering the formation of a 'Unified State Archival Fund' it was another step along the road of modernisation, establishing the Soviets as an equal with their European neighbours,[3] the Soviets were completely committed to recording their every decision. However, despite the care and devotion given to the creation and maintenance of the Soviet archives, it is doubtful that today's historians could 'scientifically' recreate the past using the evidence that the archives provide. This is not simply because today's historians employ more subtle methodology than to just accept the version of the facts that are in the archive.[4] There is plenty of evidence to tell us that the Soviets manipulated the contents of their archives (a practice not

---

1   Pankaj Mishra, 'The Mask It Wears', *London Review of Books*, 21 June 2018.
2   Blouin & Rosenberg, Processing the Past, p14-15.
3   Graziosi, Andrea. "The New Soviet Archival Sources. Hypotheses for a Critical Assessment." *Cahiers Du Monde Russe* 40, no. 1/2 (1999): 13-63. http://www.jstor.org/stable/20171117. (p14)
4   See Annie Ring, 'The (W)hole in the archive', *Paragraph*, Paragraph, Volume 37 Issue 3, p388 for brief discussion of the impact of Derrida and Foucault on the archive.

confined to the Soviets, of course) in order to present a particular aspect of the 'truth' of the situation.

There are several ways in which the Soviet archives were used to serve a particular purpose. At the mass level, staff of Soviet institutions organised and preserved everything so that decisions could later be justified – and for the individuals concerned that could be a matter of life or death. At the elite level, it was more sophisticated than a question of saving your skin. As Gregory and Harrison have observed, the most surprising thing about the archives of the Soviet leadership is that they exist at all: 'While political power and economic organisation always rested on a bedrock of informal relationships, the degree to which the exercise of power was expressed in writing is nonetheless staggering,'[5] they noted.

This line of reasoning implicitly accepts that those compiling the archives were cognisant of the fact that they were recording their own crimes – though it could also be argued that they didn't see it this way at all. Perhaps we should not be surprised about the existence of the NKVD Order no 00447 (the directive issued on July 30 1937 during the Great Terror giving extraordinary powers to the Soviet police) and similar orders within the Soviet archive because the actions were seen as necessary at the time = as baffling as that may be to us now. The archives created a powerful version of the past – but it was of course the state's version, which could sit in contrast sometimes to Soviet citizens' own memories. On a personal level Sheila Fitzpatrick has observed Stalin was himself a virtuoso of archive curating.[6]

The legacy of Lenin's 1918 decree is that, as of 1992, the Soviet archives held an estimated 138.7m files consisting of billions of individual documents. As historians when we use these files, we are conscious of the normal problems of bias present in any source along with bias in our own comprehension of those sources,

---

5   Gregory, Paul, and Mark Harrison. "Allocation under Dictatorship: Research in Stalin's Archives." *Journal of Economic Literature* 43, no. 3 (2005): 721-61. http://www.jstor.org/stable/4129474.

6   Sheila Fitzpatrick, 'Just Like That' (Review of Stalin Vol II; Waiting for Hitler, 1928-41 by Stephen Kotkin), *London Review of Books*, Vol 40, no 7, 5 April 2018, p31.

whether archival or not. What is different about archive sources is that they invite questions as to how closely they reflect the reality of the meeting or interrogation they are supposed to describe. The writers may have 'improved' the record in some way, or been tempted to fall back on using a familiar formulation in order to avoid irritating superiors with unexpected items.

We know that these problems are not unique to the Soviet archives and minutes of government department meetings have been 'tidied up' the world over. For example, in the UK, another nation obsessed with bureaucracy, a new Secretary to the Joint Intelligence Committee in the 1950s, experienced the challenges of writing minutes that reflected the spirit rather than the letter of what had actually been said. On presenting his first set of—accurate— minutes to his superior, he received the horrified reply: '… but it's absolute tripe… your job is to make the minutes readable and correct and not send out absolute nonsense.' In future, to avoid further reprimand, the Secretary made sure that any 'absolute nonsense' was omitted: 'We didn't alter them factually, we just made them sound like they were uttered by intelligent and gifted and knowledgeable people.'[7]

While much has been written on the interpretation of Soviet sources, the historiography is still lagging behind when it comes to the files of the political police.

In the literature, the debate over the Soviet political police files has several unique features. First, historians reporting these sources frequently connect with their inner anthropologist, dropping for a moment the remote narrator's persona and remarking on the impact the sources had on them as people. Lynne Viola in her study of the Ukrainian NKVD personnel notes that the files are deeply unpleasant to work with given the extensive discussion of torture that lies within.[8] Stephen Kotkin has also spoken about the trauma he underwent reading through the files for his biography of Stalin,

---

7   M. Goodman, The Official History of the Joint Intelligence Committee Volume I: From the Approach of the Second World War to the Suez Crisis, 2014, p5.
8   Lynne Viola, *Stalinist Perpetrators on Trial*, Oxford, 2017, p7.

acknowledging that prolonged periods of time of study can be up-setting: 'It's oppressive, there's no question. Imagine that there are some documents that are interrogation protocols — that is people who were beaten to confess to crimes they didn't commit — and on those documents there are lingering traces of those people's blood... And you see that again and again. It's very hard...'[9]

Secondly the debate over the archives of the Soviet political police is unusual in that basic questions — such as whether the contents of the files are true — has not been resolved with little consensus among historians. According to Hiroaki Kuromiya, the contents of the interrogation files are 'essentially fictions',[10] bearing no relation to the reality of the interrogation, and existing only as a kind of post facto justification for actions that were so extreme that they had to be documented somehow. Yet John Arch Getty contends that what is found in the interrogation files is not a stream of 'outrageous' and 'constant' lies. He argues that the situation is much more complex than this, and that what is there was written for a purpose, and with a clear objective in mind.[11] But what was this purpose and who defined the objective? This depends on the document and who was writing it. There may also have been a certain level of codification in the way that files were written. These questions focus on the interrogation file but of course there are many other files in the archives of the political police that are not interrogation files — although they may still be subject to problems of falsehood or at least embellishment but the literature remains largely silent on the question of these files.

Two aspects are specific to the examination of the interrogation files. First there are problem of their truth and authenticity (as with all historical archive sources) are magnified. Secondly, there is the specific problem of torture and the emotional aspect of dealing

---

9   The American Interest podcast, episode 184: Stephen Kotkin on Stalin, https://www.the-american-interest.com/podcast/episode-184-stephen-kotkin-stalin/ from minute 28 onwards.
10   For example, Kuromiya, H, *The Voices of the Dead: Stalin's Great Terror in the 1930s*, Yale University Press, 2007, p6-7.
11   Getty and Naumov, Yezhov biog, pxxii

with such material. To explore the files of writers who were arrested in the summer of 1937 is to find oneself brought up sharply against one glaring question: Why did the officers of the NKVD keep such detailed file notes on their prisoners, and take such care over their 'confessions'? If the 'limits' for the numbers of people to be arrested and exiled or executed were already in place, why not then just arrest the requisite number of offenders? There are a number of possible explanations.

An early interpretation was Arthur Koestler's portrayal of Bukharin in his 1940 novel *Darkness at Noon*. In this novel, Rubashov, the character representing Bukharin, makes a false confession as a last service to the Soviet state, believing that it will somehow contribute positively to the fight against fascism. But as Kuromiya points out, most of those arrested in the 1930s were not members of the Politburo and did not see their confession as a final service to Stalin.[12]

Igal Halfin's examination of interrogations of academics working at the Communist University in Leningrad used a similar argument—that ideology had been internalised to the extent that Communists began to suspect themselves. It has since been argued however that the case studies used in the book represent too narrow a section of Soviet society to be meaningfully applied to the rest of those arrested.[13]

Many of these files run to hundreds of pages and are filled with the detailed testimony of witnesses and accomplices, alongside newspaper articles, correspondence and even theatre programmes, all of which seem to help to prove the case. Yet we know that many of those accused in the 1930s were rehabilitated. The crimes were false. Guilt was a foregone conclusion and sentencing was often carried out by 'troika', which was effectively an extralegal process. If sentencing was carried out with so little regard for due process, then what was the need for such in-depth interrogation files?

---

12 Kuromiya, H, *The Voices of the Dead: Stalin's Great Terror in the 1930s*, Yale University Press, 2007, p9.
13 Yekelchyk. Socieal history, 37:3, 347-349.

So, how to approach these files, the majority of which belong not to the elite but to ordinary Soviet citizens? Historians agree that this is a difficult task. Kuromiya warned that: 'Reading these case files demands the utmost care and caution.' Getty agrees that the files must be used carefully.[14][15] Yet beyond an agreement that these files must be read with due care, there is relatively little consensus about the contents of these files and what they really signify.

Most contentious is the view that despite their reputation for heartless cruelty, the leaders of the NKVD did actually value human life and could not see it destroyed without some plausible justification. This of course suggests a level of documentary responsibility within the political police — some kind of understanding that y their actions had historical significance and warranted a record being kept. Another plausible motive for such careful and neat preservation was the need to pass the case files on to superiors in order for them to make a judgment. An extra dimension is added to this interpretation by those who have identified an element of genuine creativity in the work of the NKVD officers who created the interrogation file. So one writer has described the NKVD's interrogation files as 'a singularly powerful genre of writing...'[16] and one that actually had some impact on the Soviet writing of the time. Another describes the victims of the NKVD as 'a fictitious persona, a protagonist in a literary creation composed by the investigation team'.[17]

A further explanation is that the NKVD kept truthful and honest notes of the confessions made by those arrested; that they just wrote down what people said to them. There is evidence to suggest that those who had been arrested somehow understood the possibility of self-preservation by giving the names of those close to them to the political police.[18] Therefore it is possible that although the

---

14 Getty & Naumov, Yezhov biography, pxxii.
15 Harris JR. The Great Urals: Regionalism and the Evolution of the Soviet System.
16 Vatelescu, C, *Police Aesthetics: Literature, Film and the Secret Police in Soviet* Times, Stanford University Press, 2010, p55.
17 Halfin, I, *Stalinist Confessions: Messianism and Terror at the Leningrad Communist University*, University of Pittsburgh Press, 2009, p113.
18 See for example, Whitewood, P, *The Red Army and the Great Terror: Stalin's Purge of the Soviet Military*, University Press of Kansas, 2015, p205.

notes from the interrogations seem far-fetched, they are simply a record of the offenders' true remarks: those who had learned to 'Speak Bolshevik' now showed that they could also 'Confess Bolshevik'.

A third explanation prioritises promises and threats made to the prisoner. Promises might include fair treatment for the prisoner's family while threats no doubt meant torture, whether physical or psychological. Other aspects of the process or circumstances of interrogation fall under this heading too: those who saw their interrogation as having a therapeutic quality, and those who simply 'gabbled on' as long as they could in order to draw out time before they were sentenced.[19]

Another explanation arises when we consider the shifting nature of the political police during the 1930s. As has already been made clear, the ranks of the political police grew by several thousand members during the first half of the decade and many were then purged during the second half of the decade. This inevitably meant that officers with very little experience sometimes conducted interrogations.[20] They may have been keen to please their superiors and aware of the need for fast results. We may include, as part of this explanation, the tendency of the Soviet political police from its very beginning to rely on interrogation as its primary tool, rather than more time-consuming investigation.[21]

Regardless of which of these explanations is the most accurate, very few historians suggest that the confessions reflect genuine crimes — though Wendy Goldman suggests that while most arrests were fabricated, it is difficult to believe that absolutely everyone arrested was innocent.[22] Ultimately the length of the files means that as historians we can all find something there that we agree with or that chimes with our argument. We bring our interpretation to

---

19   Lenoe ME. The Kirov Murder and Soviet History.

20   Gregory, P, *Terror By Quota: State Security from Lenin to Stalin*, Yale University Press, 2009, p208

21   Harris, J, *The Great Fear: Stalin's Terror of the 1930s*, Oxford University Press, 2016, p33.

22   Goldman W. The Question of the Perpetrator in Soviet History. Slavic Review. Spring 2013.

these texts, just as the officers that wrote them interpreted the texts of writers, and indeed the events of their lives and the people with whom those chose to spend their time.

In the case of Ukrainian writers, a further question needs to be asked. It has been noted that Yezhov often attended the interrogations of those arrested when they took place in Moscow. He would 'bombard' Stalin with copies of the notes from the interrogations.[23] However Yezhov could not be present at the interrogations in Kiev, as he did not arrive in the city until the spring of 1938. What impact did the distance between Moscow and Kiev have on the interrogations that took place there, if any? The remainder of this chapter will ponder these questions in the context of two detailed case studies.

Case study 1: Les Kurbas

In Ukraine in the 1930s, Ukrainian nationalism was seen as a major threat to Soviet power, and this had a specific impact on the way that the repression took place there. Ukrainian intellectuals, many of whom had been at the forefront of the Ukrainian cultural resurgence of the 1920s, often found themselves accused of plotting to overthrow the Soviet authorities in the early 1930s.

One such individual was Oleksandr Stepanovich (Les) Kurbas. He was a theatre director and practitioner in Ukraine in the 1920s and now acknowledged as one of the foremost theatrical talents of his age. He was arrested towards the end of 1933 and charged with running a cell of a Ukrainian nationalist organisation. He was sentenced to five years imprisonment and executed in 1937.

Kurbas's file begins in an ominous fashion: the first page, the official record of Kurbas' arrest, has at some point been torn into four quarters, and later been taped back together. This is not the usual wear and tear that we might expect to see on documents filed roughly 80 years ago, but a very deliberate tear both horizontally

---

23   See Getty and Naumov, *Yezhov: The Rise of Stalin's "Iron Fist,"* 3-6

and vertically.[24] As such, it marks an intriguing opening to an intriguing file, suggesting that the arrest might perhaps have been temporarily overturned or abandoned.

The file itself is around 240 pages long—of which only around 100 relate to his interrogation or investigation. The cover is dated from December 1933 to April 1934 though the file contains a large amount of material from after that date, including the paperwork for his rehabilitation in the 1950s and a large amount of correspondence from the 1980s much of it from Ukrainian theatre journals trying to find out the details of his arrest and death.

The file begins

The only image of Kurbas to be found in the file appears on a commemorative envelope which contained a letter from a journalist working at a Ukrainian literary journal in 1989. The letter was addressed to the KGB and asked for information about Kurbas's arrest and death. Whoever has compiled this file has decided to keep the envelope, one of only two in the file. Perhaps this is because the journalist has written at the end of her letter 'PS Please pay attention to the envelope—it is dedicated to OS Kurbas'.

The evidence presented against Kurbas is scant, simply his own signed confession, and the testimony of four of his contemporaries all in agreement that Kurbas was fighting for Ukrainian independence. Each of these testimonies is approximately ten pages long. In this testimony, the emphasis is not on the creative work that Kurbas did as a theatre practitioner but on allegations that Kurbas used his theatre, the Berezil' Theatre in Kharkiv, as a hub for like-minded Ukrainian nationalists. This makes an interesting comparison with writers arrested in Russia in the same period, where the main focus of the charges made against them was the anti-Soviet content of their prose or poetry.

We know that the charges against Kurbas are false, not least because the second hundred pages (from the 1950s) of the file is dedicated to refuting the first hundred (from the 1930s). However, let us suspend our disbelief for a second, and imagine that we do

24   Reference? See Ukraine notebook

not know whether Kurbas's claims are true or not. The testimony against him suggests that Kurbas's main aim, as the leader of this nationalist cell, was the direct overthrow of the Soviet authorities. In the testimony on this matter, the language tends towards what we might consider as so formulaic as to indicate that it was fabricated, as we see here in the testimony from one of Kurbas's contemporaries, Mikhail Datskov discussing Ukraine in the mid-1920s: 'This new stage in the struggle against Bolshevism was characterised by a desire: to capture the top leadership of the Soviet command...'[25]

Imagine for a moment if this was genuine and that this group of Ukrainian thespians truly harboured anti-Soviet feelings. Perhaps they spoke openly about their concerns about the direction the Soviet Union was going in and maybe it even spilled over into angry rhetoric that could, in a certain light, be made to sound as if they planned to 'overthrow' the Soviet leadership. This could possibly suggest an explanation for the contents of these files: that they were not altogether false, they just stretched the truth a little.

However, if this is the case, then it is interesting to note that in this case, the interrogator stretched the truth so far but no further. In a later interrogation of another of Kurbas's contemporaries, Tkachik, it was suggested that Kurbas was involved in a plot to kill Stalin. Tkachik began by explaining Kurbas's opinion on the need for terrorism, saying: '... he explained to us the importance and necessity of terror... In Ukraine, we need to kill Balitsky, Kossior and Postishev. Gasko threw back the reply: 'Postishev is Stalin's henchman. We need to kill Stalin...' The interrogator then asks: 'Speaking of Stalin, did Gasko have any concrete proposals?'

To which Tkachik limply replies: 'He did not give any concrete proposals at this meeting.'[26] If this interrogation was a complete falsehood then either the person who concocted it had a taste for nuance or they just were not very good at their job.

Another key point from Kurbas's file is the lack of evidence of Kurbas attempting to deny the charges against him. Aside from the

25   SBU, F.6, Op.1, Spr. 75608, p14.
26   SBU, F.6, Op.1, Spr. 75608, p23.

testimony, the file is quite repetitious handwritten documents are accompanied by typewritten copies and notes and extracts from minutes appear again and again, often repeating the same or very similar information. However, although it is repetitious, it is not chaotic. Everything is ordered, the documents are all clearly laid out and even the envelopes from various bits of correspondence are saved and clipped in alongside the letters that they contained.

Case study 2: Mykola Zerov

Mykola Zerov was a leading poet in Ukraine in the 1920s and a professor of literature at Kyiv Institute of People's Education from 1923 to 1935. He was arrested by the NKVD for anti-Soviet activities in 1935 and executed in November 1937.

Although he was a member of the Ukrainian intelligentsia he occupied a different position in the intellectual landscape from Kurbas, and his interrogation file is also quite different from that of Kurbas. While the information on Kurbas's sentence and rehabilitation is all contained in one self-contradictory bundle, the information on Zerov needs seven different files, the longest of which is 300 pages. The dates of the files overlap so there is more than one file for the same period in 1935, and unlike Kurbas's file, there is a separate file for the material to do with rehabilitation in the 1950s. At 60 pages, it is also shorter than the section in Kurbas's file.

Part of the reason these files are so lengthy is that it doesn't just record information about Zerov. The title of the file is 'Zerov and others' and includes testimony and material relating to other members of Zerov's circle. There is also a lot of repetition in the files, with handwritten and typed versions of the same testimony. While Kurbas's handwriting is neat throughout his file, Zerov's handwriting shows a marked deterioration through his set of files.

File number five is dated from Jan 1935 to Sept 1935. This file has a contents page which shows that its relatively simple contents are comprised of the records of interrogation of five witnesses, some of whom are interviewed multiple times. There are fourteen different interrogations in total, as well as summaries of the cases of another five suspects. As might be expected, there is also more detail in the Zerov files, and, interestingly, by comparison to Kurbas's file there is also far greater reference to the creative and academic work of the suspects, and how this led them into the milieu of the Ukrainian nationalists. In the interrogation of one of Zerov's contemporaries, AA Zaprozhets, he admits writing the preface to a book of poetry specifically because he supported the nationalist character of the verses. Furthermore, the rather intricate network of pseudonyms both Zaprozhets and the poet Terpilovski employed in the publication of the book suggests that they knew they were involved in something that might be problematic.

The interrogator asks: 'Did you write a preface to the poems written by Terpilovski... and with what name did you sign this preface?' Zaprozhets answers that he had met Terpilovski while on holiday in the summer of 1934, and goes on to explain: 'When I met him, I found out that he wrote poems. These poems had a clearly pronounced Ukrainian nationalist character. Myself as a Ukrainian nationalist liked them very much...' He admitted writing the preface explaining that he signed it with the surname Zadunaisky because: 'Zadunaisky is my pseudonym. Subsequently, I changed the alias Zadunaisky to Oles' Chaika.Terpilovsky in turn had a pseudonym M.O. Vizvol'nii... subsequently replaced by the pseudonym Pavlo Gaidarenko. Therefore, my preface was devoted to the analysis of the ideological direction of creativity of M.O. Vizvol'nii.'[27]

File number one, which overlaps with the fifth file in terms of time, also has detail about the professional activities of the suspects. For example, one suspect describes giving lectures about Ukrainian literature, and how this led on to his becoming a member of a counter-revolutionary organisation.[28] During the interrogations with Zerov in this file, there is also a lot more evidence of Zerov denying the charges against him. At one point he is interrogated face-to-face with another suspect, Pilipovich. At the opening of the interrogation, they are both asked to identify each other. Pilipovich does identify Zerov, and adds that Zerov was the leader of a counter-

27   Zerov, file 5, p19
28   Zerov, file 5, p204.

revolutionary organisation, but Zerov says he does not know Pilipovich. Later in the interrogation, Pilipovich says that he met Zerov at the beginning of 1934, and that as they got to know each other they began to discuss political topics, and eventually Zerov began to talk about counter-revolutionary organisation and their methods of work. The interrogator asks Zerov whether he will confirm this information, but he simply answers: 'I do not confirm.'[29]

In this file the repetitive nature of the interrogation style becomes clear, as the interrogator asks the suspect to repeat statements made in earlier interrogations over and over again. At one point it seems that Zerov loses patience with this technique, as he snaps: 'What I've said about counter-revolutionary activity has already been said.'[30]

Conclusion: making sense?

The contrast highlighted by Katerina Clark between the fantastical nature of the testimony and meticulous way the files were transcribed and preserved is manifestly clear. As with so many archive files, there is a danger that we go to them and find what we believed we would find. However, and with this in mind, the first conclusion from these files is that, as Clark hints, the great length and detail of the files has very little to do with prosecuting the case against the suspect—whose fate was in effect already decided. So if it was not a file in that sense, what was it? Some historians have suggested that the files are a complete falsehood but this does not seem to be the case with these files—or how else would we explain Zerov's refusal to co-operate in the face-to-face interrogation?

What is also clear is that despite massive structural and bureaucratic upheaval within the Ukrainian NKVD at this time, the files are clear, logical and well organised. Some have suggested that these files were created in order to clearly document how and when decisions were made as a form of self-protection, although if this was the strategy then Lynne Viola's recent book suggests that it did not work as over 20 per cent of the NKVD staff were themselves

---

29   Zerov, file 1, p134-135.
30   Ibid, 194.

purged in 1939 after Stalin called a halt to the purges, despite the evidence of the interrogation files[31] However, as these operatives could not have seen what the future held, we should not totally discount the motive of wanting to document carefully the guilt of each suspect. Indeed, it is tempting to suggest that while the purges raged, and bureaucratic chaos was rife throughout the republic, these files were the one space in which logic and order reign.

What also transpires from these files is the difficulty of making generalisations about them. The admissions of guilt do not follow a pattern: some suspects did admit their 'guilt' and others put up a fight. There are varying levels of emphasis between the cultural credentials of the suspects and their Ukrainian nationalism within the two files. Although these files are from a similar time, and the subjects come from similar backgrounds and are charged with similar crimes, nevertheless we can see that the two cases have subtle but important differences. Rather than one over-arching explanation for the existence and the length and tangled logic of these files, in fact it is probably more likely that we will find the explanation(s) in the specific suspects themselves, and beyond that in the circumstances and events of Ukraine in the 1930s: a badly functioning NKVD, under huge pressure to complete a task of mammoth proportions, with a staff sometimes made up of young and inexperienced officers who needed to document all their decisions carefully.

When Sheila Fitzpatrick was choosing a topic for her postgraduate studies, she tried to avoid anything too 'Shapiro-like'.[32] Included in this category was the political police of the Soviet Union under Stalin, known as the OGPU and later as the NKVD. It was thought that this topic was simply too totalitarian to make a good topic for an author so committed to demonstrating the complexity of Soviet life. The political police were too simple, they were too successful, they were just too good at what they did to be useful to a revisionist historian, wanting to get away from the clichés of Stalin as puppet-master.

---

31   Viola, *Stalinist Perpetrators on Trial*
32   See Fitzpatrick, *A Spy in the Archives*.

This study will demonstrate that Fitzpatrick was correct—the political police were exceptionally successful, efficient and ruthless in their actions throughout the 1930s. However, it will also go on to demonstrate that all this does not signify that the organisation was free of the complexity that Fitzpatrick and her colleagues have identified in so many other aspects of Soviet society. While it was a highly effective organisation, it was not well run. As has been shown here, it was prone to chaos, and to wasteful bureaucracy and high levels of upheaval with an effect on the purges that characterised much of the 1930s, and the Great Terror of the mid-late 1930s.

М. ZEРОВ

АНТОЛОГІЯ

МИКОЛА ЗЕРОВ

АНТОЛОГІЯ

РИМСЬКОЇ ПОЕЗІЇ

КАТУЛЛ · ВЕРГІЛІЙ · ГОРАЦІЙ ·
ПРОПЕРЦІЙ · ОВИДІЙ ·
МАРЦІЯЛ

Вид. Т-во „ДРУКАРЬ" — Київ
М С М Х Х.

В. К. Прокоповичу
на знак пошани
і приязні.

КАТУЛЛ, 3.

ПЛАЧ, Венеро! плачте, Купідони!
Плачте, люде витончені й чемні:
Вмер горобчик милої моєї,
Вмер горобчик, що вона любила
І як свого ока доглядала.
Був він ніжний і ласкаву пані
Знав, як доня малолітня матір:
На її колінах завжди бавивсь
І, стрибаючи навколо неї,
Щебетанням вірним озивався.
А тепер і він пішов до краю,
Звідкіля ніхто ще не вертався...
Хай во віки ти не діждеш долі,
Попідземна темряво несита!
Ти нам радість нашу відібрала...
Горе й нам, горобчику сердечний!
Через тебе дорогі очиці
Од плачу, од сліз почервоніли.

АВРЕЛІЙ і Фурій — Катуллові друзі:
    Куди-б не пішов він, ви тими-ж стежками —
На море Індійське, що рве і бурхає
     В бою з берегами —

До саків далеких — до ніжних арабів —
Між парти, стрільців племено гострозоре —
В Єгипет пекучий, де Нілові гірла
     Замулили море...

Поглянули-б з ним ви й за гори Альпійські —
В долини, де Цезарь прославивсь великий,
На Рейн пограничний і острів Британський
     Далекий і дикий.

І все, що-б там Доля мені не послала,
Зо мною ви радо усе б поділили!...
Тож прошу моїй передати коханій
     Це слово немиле:

Дай боже їй жити й повік процвітати
І триста коханців водити з собою,
І серце їх бідне лукавою тільки
      В'ялити жагою.

Моєї-ж любови вона не діждеться:
Кохання Катуллове вмерло, – упало,
Як квіт польовий, коли пройде по ньому
      Залізнеє рало.

КАТУЛЛ, 26.

НАШ дім поставлений в куточку затишному:
Ні Австр, ні Апельйот не рушать мого дому;
Фавоній і Борей дихнуть не сміють там,—
А вітру все таки не сила збутись нам:
Наш дім заставлений за двісті тисяч, Фуре!
О пагубо моя, боргів шалена буре!

ХЛОПЧИСЬКУ слуго! давнього Фалерну
Подай нам чашу пінну та гірку!
Такий наказ Постумії-цариці,
П'янішої від п'яних виногрон.
Ти-ж, пагубо вина—твереза водо,
Ти йди від нас до мудрих та розважних:
Тут нерозведений панує Вакх.

ЗНОВУ весна, оживає земля.
Бурь одгреміла пора буркотлива,
З заходу легіт повіяв пестливий...
Де ви, багатої Фрігії ниви?
Де ти, Никеї родюча рілля?...
В Азію, славну містами, мчимо.
Серце забилося, прагне дороги,
Радо ступають, тугішають ноги...
Друзі, прощайте! братерським гуртком
З дому забились ми в даль незнайому,—
Нарізно шлях свій верстаєм до-дому.

ВЕРГІЛІЙ.
I еклога.

Мелібей:

ТИТИРЕ, ти в холодку опочив-єсь під буком
[гіллястим
І на сопілці сільській награєш мелодійної пісні.
Ми-ж потишили наш дім, наші ниви; од рідного
[краю
Геть утікаєм... Нам тяжко.. А ти — в холодку, на
[дозвіллі
Будиш в діброві луну солодким ім'ям Амарілли.

Титир:

О, Мелібею! мій бог послав мені втіху цю й радість.
Завжди для мене лишиться він богом; олтарь його
[завжди
Буде окроплено кров'ю ягнятка з моєї кошари:
З ласки його бо на пашу корів я й ягнят виганяю,
З ласки його награю, що захочу, на тихій сопілці.

Мелібей:

Так! Я не заздрю тобі... Я дивуюсь... Бо ж буря лютує
Нині на наших ланах. І сам я, старий та безсилий,

Кіз своїх далі жену... А ця? поглянь бо на неї:
Двох на горбі козенят у ліщині вона породила,
Так і лишила їх мертвими там, на камінні неплиднім.
Часто це лихо мені—о моя сліпота та нерозум!—
Громом розбиті дуби на путі на моїй віщували;
Часто це горе гірке вороння накликало зловісне...
Але хто-ж бог твій і де він, скажи мені, Титире
[друже?

Т и т и р :

В Римі мій спас і заступник... ти знаєш, простець
[незвичайний,
Місто те дивне, гадав я, подібне до наших містечок,
Де на базарах ми сир продавали і наші ягниці;
Думав я: пес, хоч і більший, у всьому подібний
[щенятам.
Нині я знаю, що Рим над містами підноситься всіми,
Як над кущами повзкої лози кипарис величавий.

М е л і б е й :

Що-ж так манило тебе до того величнього міста?

Т и т и р :

Воля, мій друже! Хоч пізно, як волос на старість
[посивів,
Взнав я принади її, — осяяла вік мій ледачий;
Зглянулась доля на мене, хоч довго прийшлось її
[ждати.

Перш Галатеїн невільник, я нині служу Амариллі...
От як була Галатея, то — щиро тобі признаюся:
Вільної хвилі не мав я, не мав заробітку ніколи...
Хоч на олтарь і складав я нелічені жертви безсмертним,
Хоч працював я, як міг, і сир свій видавлював туго,
З грішми ніколи моя не верталась до дому правиця.

Мелібей:

От коли я зрозумів, чому так Амарілла зітхала,
Щиро молилась богам, для кого виноград зберігала:
Титир покинув свій дім—а по ньому тут сосни

[журились
І говіркі джерела, і широкі зелені діброви.

Титир:

Що-ж мені діять було? Чи-ж я міг зоставатися в

[призрі?
Чи-ж я не міг попросити у бога спокою та пільги?..
О, Мелібею! я бачив там мужа, що йому на шану
Пишні що-місяця жертви по храмах приносяться

[наших;
І на благання своє ласкаву почув я одповідь:
Все, що твоє, при тобі! Вертайсь до худоби безпечно!

Мелібей:

О, ти щасливий, мій друже! Майно і твій хутір з

[тобою.
Досить тобі на життя .. Твоє поле оброблене добре...

Не заболочений луг: ні комиш, ні рогіз не росте там.
Не на чужому ти пастимеш вівці, і пошесть ворожа
Од незнайомих сусід на ягнята твої не перейде.
Так! ти щасливий, мій друже! Ти дома, лежиш в
[холодочку
Біля священих джерел, на березі рідної річки.
Тут тобі тин-живопліт, де гіблейські трудівниці
[бжоли
Взяток важенний беруть на буйнім верболозовім цвіті,
Вколо літають, бренять, до солодкого сну запрошають;
Тут, по-під скелю йдучи, садівничий наспівує пісні;
Тут про кохання твоє голуби тобі стиха туркочуть
І з верховіття кленка озивається горлиця ніжна...

Титир:

Так, мені добре... І перше олень піде пастись в
[повітря,
Море раніше всі викине риби на піски безвідні,
Парти із жизних долин приблукають раніше до Рейну,
А напівдикий германець Евфратові питиме води,—
Аніж у серці моїм захитається образ владики.

Мелібей:

Лихо судилося нам; ми йдемо на безвіддя Лібійські,
Другі мандрують до скитів, а треті—на берег Оакси;
Навіть на північ, за море ідуть до Британського
[краю...
Чи й доведеться коли повернутися знов до отчизни,

Щоби з слізьми на очах, по роках сумного вигнання,
Глянуть на землю свою, на ту стріху убогої хати.
Жовнір захожий мої родючі виснажить ниви,
Варвар тут жатиме хліб... От до чого усобиця люта
Нас, громадян, довела!... Чи для того ходив я за
                                        [полем,
Чи за-для того я груші щепив і викохував лози?...
Кози, щасливі колись, годі плакатись,—далі рушаймо!
Вже не лежати мені по-між рястом у темній печері,
Вже не дивитись на вас, по далекій розсипаних скелі,
Пісні уже не співати, і певно, що скоро без мене
Вам доведеться гіркий верболіз та конюшину скубти.

                    Титир:

Ні, ти не підеш нікуди і ніч перебудеш зо мною;
Ложем нам буде трава, а вечерю ми маєм розкішну:
Добре оддавлений сир, і каштани, і яблука спілі.
Глянь бо: ген-ген над хатами димок уже в'ється
                                        [вечірній
І од гірських верховин по долинах послалися тіни.

ВЕРГІЛІЙ.
IV еклога.

МУЗИ Сициліі! нині почнем поважнішої пісні;
Кущ тамариску, гаї та діброви не всім до вподоби:
Вже як співать про ліси, хай той спів буде консула
[гідний.

Час надіходить останній по давніх пророцтвах
[кумейських;
Низка щасливих віків на землі починається знову.
Знову вертається Діва, вертається царство Сатурна;
Парость новітню богів нам із ясного послано неба.

Ти лише, чиста Діяно, злелій нам дитину ту дивну:
З нею залізна доба переходить, спадає в непам'ять,
Вік настає золотий! Непорочна, твій Феб уже з нами!

Так! і у твій консулят, Полліоне, це станеться чудо,
Місяці дивні, щасливі літа розпочнуться від тебе:
Щезнуть останні сліди диких чварів і братньої крови,
Від неснастанних трівог земля одпочине страдденна.

18

Хлопчику любий! надійдуть часи, і побачиш ти небо,
Світлих героїв побачиш і сам засіяєш в їх колі,
Правлячи світом усім, втихомиреним зброєю батька.

Зразу-ж родюча земля принесе тобі перші дарунки:
Ладан поземний та кручений плющ зростить без
                                        [насіння,
Лотосом вся процвіте, засміється веселим акантом.
Кози самі понесуть молоко з полонини додому;
Смирна худоба без страху на лева глядітиме в полі.
Квіти ласкаві, рясні поростуть край твоєї колиски.
Згине і ворог твій—змій і все зілля отрутне загине
І асирійський амом ніби килимом землю укриє.

Виростеш ти і почнеш дізнаватись про славу героїв,
Батькову славу пізнаєш і мужности міць непохитну,
Колосом буйно-важким заговорять лани неосяжні.
Терна колючого кущ зчервоніє від грон виноградних.
Листя суворих дубів золотистим ороситься медом.

Де-що лишиться проте із давніших гріхів та нещастя.
Випливуть в море човни, і місто оточиться муром;
Рало по лону землі борозною глибокою пройде.
З'явиться Тифис новий, і юнацтво добірне, одважне
Славну збудує Арго і в кріваві походи полине.
З смілим лицарством Ахилл проти нової вирушить
                                        [Трої.

Мужем ти станеш і віку дозрілого дійдеш,—чи бачиш:
В морі не видко вітрил, і сосни нагірні не возять
Краму по хвилях морських; все, що треба, земля дає
[людям.
Оранки більше нема, ні ножа для кущів виноградних;
Скинув волові ярмо з терпеливої шиї плугатарь.

Вовни не красять уже у фарби, пороблені штучно:
Нині вівця на пасовищі ходить в одежі червленій,
Кольором ясним шафрана та пурпуром мініться
[темним;
Нині природний сандикс одягає ягнят недорослих.

Дивні надходьте віки! До своїх веретен нахилившись,
Присуд сповняючи Долі, так випряли Парки нехибні.

Час вже обняти тобі руками дитячими владу,
Вибранче милий богів, Юпітера славний нащадку!
Глянь, як на радости всесвіт дріжить, як радість
[проймає
Море і простір землі, і безодню глибокого неба;
Глянь, як подвиглось усе назустріч прийдешнього віку.

О коли-б мав я на світі прожить і, як пан свого хисту,
Співом прославить гучним твої вчинки для пізніх
[нащадків!

Проти мене не устояв тоді-б ні Орфій-Ісмарієць,
Ані досвідчений Лін, хоч обом їм боги помагали —
Калліопея Орфію, а Лінові Феб уродливий.
Навіть і Пан, коли став-би зо мною до суду аркадців,
Навіть і Пан-чарівник признав-би мою перемогу!

Хлопчику любий! навчися-ж вітати всміхаючись матір:
Болю і прикрих страждань довелось їй натерпітись
[досить.
Хлопчику любий, навчися! Кого бо не пестила мати,
Той не зазнав ні поваги богів, ні кохання богині.

ВЕРГІЛІЙ.
Енеїда, V, 835-871.

ТЕМРЯВА ночі уже досягала середини неба;
   Тяжко стомились гребці, і, знесилені, кинули
                       [весла
Та на помості мулкім та по лавах твердих полягали.
Тільки спочили, як Сон лехкокрилий з етеру ясного
Вохким повітрям летить і тумани нічні розгортає.
Так, Палінуре, він лине до тебе, — зловісні примари
Він насилає на зір твій... Он сів він на кермі висòко,
Образ Форбанта прийнявши, і з словом до тебе
                           [вдається:
„Язидів сину, поглянь: — самі хвилі пильнують за тебе,
Рівно так дише повітря, — настала година спокою.
Голову ти прихили, дай спочити натруженим очам, —
Я замісць тебе посижу, за хвилею й морем догляну.“
Ледве підводячи вії, натомлений мовить стерничий:
„Що мені радиш, Форбанте? Невже ж я довірюсь
                           [потворі?
Чи, ти гадаєш, не знаю я хвилі облудного моря?
Як доручу їй Енея; досвідчений давній керманич,
Мало я бачив біди од погідного неба та моря?“
Так одмовляв він, — спокійно і міцно тримався кормила,

І не одводив очей од зір на високому небі.
Взяв Лехкокрилий тоді галузку, обмочену в Леті
Й міццю снотворною Стикса напоєну, й чоло старого
Стиха обвіяв. Одразу-ж по кволому тілу розлився
Непереможний спокій; склепились досвідчені очі.
Знявшись угору тоді і на човен упавши звисока,
Бог одриває стерно і скидає стерничого в море, —
Марне кричав Палінур, марне в друзів благав
                                    [порятунку;
Бог лехкокрилий, як птах, злетів і щез у повітрі.

Мирно тим часом пливли кораблі по широкому морю.
Мирно дрімали гребці, забезпечені словом Нептуна.
І наближались уже до бескетів Сирен, до тих білих
Скель лиховістних, засіяних густо кістьми мореходців,
І зачували здалека, як бухає море о камінь...
Глянув на керму Еней і побачив: нема Палінура!
Сів до стерна і повів корабель свій по темрявих
                                    [хвилях,
Тяжко зітхаючи й сльози ллючи над недолею друга:
„О Палінуре, для чого довірився ти небові й морю,
Будеш лежать, непохований, ти на пісках невідомих.“

ГОРАЦІЙ.
Оди I, 11.

НЕГОЖЕ нам, о Левконоє, знати
Яку нам суджено в життю наземнім путь;
Халдейських віщунів не будем ми шукати:
Халдейських чисел нам, мій друже, не збагнуть.
Чи добре житимем, чи скоро час розстання —
Приймаймо з дякою, що Доля нам дає,
Хоч може ця зіма для нас зіма остання,
І вже не чутимем, як море в беріг б'є.
Розумна завжди будь. Важкий і пінний келих
До вохких уст своїх бездумно підіймай,
І безліч днів живи безжурних та веселих,
І лиш на це життя надію покладай.
Минає хутко час. Лови, лови хвилини.
Не вірь прийдешньому, що нам назустріч лине.

ГОРАЦІЙ.
Оди I, 32.
До ліри.

ПРОСЯТЬ нас і ждуть. І коли не марно
Награвали ми, коли рік і більше
Житиме наш спів, — на латинський голос
    Грай мені, ліро!

На Лесбосі вперше озвався спів твій:
Там Алкей, співець і невтомний воїн,
Як пригонить часом на вохкий берег
    Човен розбитий, —

На твоїй струні Афродиту славив,
Славив Вакха й Муз, пустуна Ерота
Й Ліка-хлопчака темнооку вроду
    Й кучері чорні.

Феба дивний дар, на бенкетах Зевса
Всім бажаний гість і в трудах щоденних
Пільга й супокій — на моє благання —
    Ліро, озвися!

ГОРАЦІЙ.
Оди I, 38.

НЕ ЛЮБЛЮ я, хлопче, роскошів перських.
Не кохаюсь я в тих вінках квітчастих, —
Не шукай по саду:—де ще зостались
        Пізні троянди?

Досить, хлопче, з нас і простого мирту:
Миртовий вінок тобі личить, слуго,
Личить і мені, коли п'ю в садочку
        Кубок веселий.

ГОРАЦІЙ.
Оди II, 3.

В ГОДИНИ розпачу умій себе стримати
І в хвилі радости заховуй супокій
І знай: однаково прийдеться умірати,
  О Деллію коханий мій, —

Чи весь свій довгий вік провадитимеш в тузі,
Чи лежачи в траві, прикрашений вінком,
Рої понурих дум на затишному лузі
  Фалерським гнатимеш вином...

Для чого-ж нам сосна й тополя білокора
Прослали по землі гостинний холодок?
По що на лузі нам наспівує прозорий
  І гомонить дзвінкий струмок?—

Вина і пахощів і ясних рож без краю—
Короткочасний цвіт!—несіть туди, несіть,
І хай дзвенить бенкет, покіль твій вік буяє
  І невблаганна Парка спить.

Бо прийде, прийде час: покинеш поле й луки,
І вілу, і сади, де Тибр тече мутний,
І на усі скарби пожадливії руки
    Наложить спадкоємець твій.

І чи в достатку жив, а чи не мавши дому
Тяжким шляхом тобі судилося пройти,
Кінець однаковий: Плутонові грізному
    Рокований на жертву ти.

І всі ми будем там. Надійде мить остання
І в човен кине нас, як діждемо черги,
І хмуро стрінуть нас довічного вигнання
    Понурі береги

ГОРАЦІЙ.
Оди III, 26.

Чи то-ж давно дівчат я чарував собою
І добрим вояком в безкровнім був бою?
А нині — вислужену зброю
І бàрбітон богині оддаю.

Сюди, сюди до ніг народженої з піни
Складайте, браття, з лівої руки —
Ліхтарь мій, що розгонив тіни,
І кий, що розбивав замки.

А ти, прославлена в південному Мемфисі,
Перед твоїм ясним схиляюсь я лицем,
Молю, Кипридо: розмахнися
Над Хлоєю святим бичем.

ЗБІГЛИ струмками сніги... Зазеленіли долини,
      Закучерявився ліс.
В новім убранні земля, і ріки, що в повінь греміли,
      В ложе вертаються знов.

Грації й нимфи, одкинувши шати й серпанки прозорі,
      Йдуть у веснянім танку...
Все на землі перемінне — так кажуть нам роки текучі
      Й сутінь померклого дня.

Тільки повіє весною, і літо уже на порозі:
      Літо перейде — і глянь:
Осінь розсипала овочі стиглі; за осінню слідом
      Мертва ступає зіма.

Місяця круг защербиться і знову пливе, повновидий —
      Смертним віднови нема.
В темнім житлі, де владика Еней, де Анк і Гостилій
      Будем ми — порох і тінь.

Хто тобі скаже, докинуть чи ні тобі боги всевишні
            Ще один завтрашній день?...
Тож потішай свою душу! не хочеш, то візьме нащадок
            Спадки незбуті твої.

А як умер ти, і Мінос-суддя проказав урочисто
            Праведний присуд тобі,
Вже не воскреснеш, Торквате! безсила побожність
                        [і рід твій,
            І красномовство твоє!

Бо від підземної тьми не звільнила свого Іпполіта
            Навіть Діяна сама,
Навіть могутній Тезей не подужав зірвать з Піритоя
            Вічних Аідових пут.

ГОРАЦІЙ.
Сатири II, 6.

ТІЛЬКИ і мрії було, — щоби клаптик малесенький
[поля,
Дім, огород і криниця з веселим струмком біля дому,
А на узгіррю, над домом, лісок... Та боги милосердні
Більше і краще послали, і ліпшого я не жадаю,
Тільки, Меркурію, ти закріпи мій маєток за мною.
Я бо не збільшив його ні крутійством, ні здирством
[безбожним,
Я і не зменшу його марнотратством та власним
[недбальством;
Я ні хвилини не думав, щоб той або инший куточок
До володіння свого приорати і вирівнять межі;
Жадних скарбів не збірав, не мріяв: „От горщика з
[сріблом
Випадком в полі знайти-б і, приязнь Ґеракла здобувши,
Стати як власник он той, що у наймах колись
[побивався.“
Я задоволений з того, що маю; я прошу одного:
„Боже! пошли, щоб худоба моя (аби тільки не розум!)
Сита була і гладка і ласкою щасна твоєю.“

Наче в твердині якій, я на хуторі в горах укрився,
Що ж тут знайти для сатир і для пішої музи моєї?
Не дошкуляють тут нас ані Австер, ні те честолюбство,
Ані пропасниці люті, ні смерти осінній ужинок.

Боже досвітніх годин, ти, що Янусом зватись волієш!
З тебе веліли безсмертні всі справи й труди починати,
З тебе щоденна моя починається пісня в столиці.
Вдосвіта ти коло ліжка: „Вставай! ти-ж, здається, за
                                           [когось
Маєш ручитись в суді, поспішай, щоб тобі не
                                           [спізнитись.“
І чи то там Аквилон розлютився, чи то в сніговиці
День найкоротший світає поволі, а треба вставати,
Бігти, розштовхувать натовп, трудитись ліктями й
                                           [плечима,
Щоби, добувшись до суду, „виразно“ зложити заяву.
Тут і на мене гукають прохожі: „Чи ти божевільний,
Чи в невідкладній потребі спішиш, — на людей не
                                           [зважаєш?
А чи ти думкою вже в Меценатових світлих хоромах?“
Меду солодші для мене слова ті... Та тільки зійду я
На Есквилин, як одразу-ж, мов хвилі, і в боки
                                           [заб’ються,
І полетять через голову тисячі справ. — „Постріваи
                                           [лиш,
Росцій просив тебе бути у претора... завтра, о другій“.—
„Скріби на збори тебе закликають... є справи важливі;
Квінте, гляди-ж, не забудь 1 не спізнюйся“! — „Любий!

Ти ублагай Мецената, нехай лиш печатку поставить!"
Скажеш: „Гаразд, я попробую". Ні! він настоює,
                                        [молить.

Сьомий минає вже рік з того часу, як ти, Меценате,
Вперше мене зачислив до свого найтіснішого кола: -
Подорожуючи, став запрошати до власної реди,
Щоби було з ким в путі перекинутись словом
                                        [незначним,
„Котра година"? спитати, чи „хто з гладіяторів
                                        [кращий?"
Або згадати, що „ранком годиться тепліш одягатись."
І хоча речі такі ти довірити всякому можеш,
Я відтоді і до нині, що-дня. що-години, то більше
З заздрощів клятих не маю спокою. На Марсовім полі
Грав ти зо мною в м'яча: „Щасливий!" зітхають
                                        [навколо.
Пройде по ринку якась поголоска, аж жах розбіра,
Всяк, хто не стрінеться, зразу-ж до мене. питається:
                                        [„Друже!
Ти в тім вельможному колі, як свій, і ти знаєш
                                        [напевно,
Що там чувати продаків?"—„Не знаю".—„Ах, завжди
                                        [ладен ти
З нас глузувати".—„Та хай мене бог покарає,—не
                                        [знаю".
Стрінеться другий: „Не чув ти, де має нарізати
                                        Цезарь
Землю своїм ветеранам, в Італії, а чи де·инде?"

Я присягаюсь, не вірять; ззираються мов би на диво:
Он вам, погляньте, зразок, як уміють ховать таємниці.

Так і марнується день. А що-вечора в серці молитва:
Хуторе мій, та коли-ж я вернуся до тебе, коли-ж я
В давніх рукописах, сні і яснім безтурботнім дозвіллі
Той пожаданий знайду одпочинок од гамору й руху?
Як і коли родичів Пітагора—боби я побачу
І біля них на столі огородинку, салом прилиту?
Ночі блаженні, вечері богів, коли давнім звичаєм
Я й мої гості їмо перед ларом, а челядь проворна
Тим, що зосталось, живиться. П'ємо, та немає ніяких
Правил у нас божевільних, і кожний п'є по охоті.
Цей почувається в силі,—міцніше вино вибірає,
Той попиває легеньке. Помалу зринає розмова,
Та не про те, що там діється в нас, по сусідніх
                                        [господах,
І не про те, як танцює Лепор. Обмірковуєм завжди
Речі поважні, що всіх нас обходять і завжди на мислі:
В чому покладено щастя, в чеснотах душі чи маєтку
Що нас принаджує в дружбі: правдива любов, чи
                                        [вигоди,
Що є найвищим добром і де грані доброго й злого.

Цервій, мій добрий сусіда, при кожній щасливій
                                        [нагоді
Нас научає байками. Як стануть Ареллія славить
За нещисленні скарби, він подумає й так починає:
„Раз мишенятко сільське, повідають, приймало міського

35

Й щиро його, по-хазяйськи, в убогій норі частувало.
Завжди ощадне, скупе, воно порішило цим разом
Справити бучний бенкет і для гостя свого дорогого
Не пожаліло ні зернят вівса, ні запасів гороху,
Витягло навіть кишмиш і шматочок надгризений сала,
Ріжноманітністю страв догодити бажаючи гостю,
Що, гордовитий, ледви доторкався тих ласощів
                                        [сільських.
Гість гидував, а господар, на свіжій прилігши
                                        [полові,
Ввічливо сам споживав лиш кукіль лихий та голодний.
Зрештою гість не втримався: „Скажи, що тебе
                                        [спокушає,
Брате мій, жити отут на узліссі, в ярах та по горах?
Чи ти волієш звірів лісових, ніж міське товариство?
Слухай, ходімо зо мною: наш вік, само знаєш,
                                        [короткий,
І нічому земнородному не врятуватись од смерти.
Тож хоч живімо, як слід: поки нашого віку,
                                        [втішаймось
Скороминущим життям; пам'ятаймо, що далі—могила".
Ці красномовні слова прийшлись до вподоби
                                        [сільському,—
Помандрувало за гостем у світ той принадний. Чималу
Путь перейшли вони, поки захоплені, раді, спинились
Перед міською стіною. Вже ночі тьмяна колесниця
Стала як раз на середині неба, коли мишенята
Розташувались в заможному домі, де килими пишні
Пурпуром ясним горіли по ложах слонової кости.

Сила недоїдків там од вечері лишилось по мисках,
Що оддалік визирали з кошів так ласкаво і смачно.
Посадовивши сільське мишеня на червленім покрові,
Ніби той раб підперезаний, заметушився господарь.
Страви без краю почав подавати і, зовсім як слуги,
Навіть прилизував їх крадькома, несучи до їдальні.
Тішиться наше село, що дізналося щастя такого;
Весело й чемно сидить, мов на справжнім бенкеті,—
                                                    [як раптом
Скрип: одчинилися двері, і миші летять на підлогу.
Жах їх несвітський пройняв: забігали скрізь по покою
І... як умерли нараз: на дворі обізвались вівчарки.
Ледве прийшовши до тямки, сільське мишенятко
                                                    [сказало:
„Ні, не для мене цей дім і життя... Прощавай! Я волію
Жити в безпечній норі і злиденним живитись горохом“.

ПРОПЕРЦІЙ.
Елегії III, 2.

КАЖУТЬ, Орфею, що ти звірів зачаровував співом
  І зупиняв течію диких тракійських струмків;
Скелі з гірських верховин, порушені струнами ліри,
  Йшли у долину до Теб — на підмурівок до стін;
Навіть на голос твоїх, Поліфеме, пісень — Галатея
  Гнала з блакитних глибин коней до Етни морських,—
Тож не здивуймо і ми, що, надиханий Вакхом і Фебом,
  Натовпи ніжних дівчат спів зачаровує мій.
Вбога оселя моя: там не знайдеш колон Тенарійських,
  Ні сволоків костяних, ні золочених склепінь;
Сад мій, малий та звичайний, не рівня гаям Феакійським:
  Штучних нема там печер, ні водограїв дзвінких,—
Музи проте не тікають од мене, читач мій зо мною,
  І Калліопі самій хори мої до душі.
Щастя, дівчино, твоє, що прославлена ти в моїй книзі,
  Кожна бо пісня моя пам'ятник вроді твоїй!
Бо-ж піраміди царів, що до зір досягають високих,
  Зевса Елейського храм — наслідування небес —
І незрівняна краса намогильного дому Мавзола
  Мають зазнать на собі смерти суворий закон.

Дощ та з'їдливий огонь підточать їх славу всесвітню;
    Роки ударять на них — порохом стануть вони,
Але не згине во-вік та слава, що геній придбає,
    Подвигів духа во-вік сяє нетлінна краса.

МАТИ Ахилла й Мемнона обидві дітей оплакали:
   Навіть великих богинь горе стріває в житті,—
Так розпускай-же і ти, жалібнице Елегіє, коси:
   Надто правдиво звучить нині наймення твоє!
Вмер твій коханий співець, твій Тибулл, твоя слава й
                                          [окраса:
   Он на високім кострі тіло бездушне його.
Син Афродити за ним з сайдаком виступає порожнім,
   Зломаний лук у руці і смолоскіп без огню,—
Бачиш, як смутно іде, опустивши знесилені крила,
   Як його ніжна рука в груди розпучливо б'є;
Як поспадали з чола його кучері ніжні на шию,
   І на рожевих устах стогін одчаю завмер.
Так, повідають, тужив він, як брата Енея ховали;
   З гірким виходив плачем з дому, Іюле, твого.
Мати Венера сама, повідають, так не тужила
   З часу, як любий юнак, вепром поранений, впав.
Кажуть: „безсмертні співці... богове піклуються вами,
   Божеська влада і міць в вашому слові живе",—

Але з'являється смерть і дочасно руйнує святиню
    І накладає на нас руки невидні свої.
Не врятували Орфея-співця ні батько, ні мати,
    Ні незрівняний його дар чарувати звірів;
В нетрях загинув і Лін, його брат по мистецтву і
                                        [крови,
    Й довго звучала в гаях Фебова пісня по нім.
А Меонид, Меонид, джерело невсихаюче співу,
    Роси святих Пієрид, спраглих потіха сердець!
В чорнім Аверні й його поглинула година остання,
    Тільки й лишивсь на землі спів невмірущий його.
В людському серці живе бідування нещасної Трої
    І Пенелопина шерсть, наново ткана у день.
Так Немезиса твоя, твоя Делія житимуть вічно,
    Пам'ять про першу твою і про останню любов;
Їх не розважать ні жертви, ні звуки єгипетських
                                        [систрів,—
    Вже не потішить ніщо ложа самотного їх.
Але як гине отак все найкраще у нас, найдорожче,—
    В серці розпука встає: „де ви, безсмертні боги?"
Свято живеш — умираєш, шануєш богів милосердних —
    А невблаганна уже смерть розкладає вогонь;
Можеш віддатись пісням — але поглянь на Тибулла:
    В урні тісній і малій ляже великий співець!
Чей-же, співаче, тебе охопило те полум'я люте:
    Вже не страшиться воно вижерти серце твоє!..

ДОСИТЬ було-б і п'яти... Шість книжок, чи там
[сім—забагато.
Музо! невже·ж це тобі ще не остило співать?
Годі! встидаймось! мовчім! Про славу ту людську не
[дбаймо:
Досить того, що і так скрізь перечитують нас.
Он од надгробку Мессали розкиданий камінь лишиться,
Порохом стане сипким мармур Ліціна твердий,
А незрадливий читач не забуде мене, і мандрівник,
Ідучи з Риму, мене візьме в свій рідний куток.
Так я промовив, мовчу. А в одежі схилившись
[пахучій,
Чую: дев'ята з сестер одповідає мені:
„Так? ти покинеш, невдячний, складать свої вірші
[веселі?
Будеш без діла сидіть, світ і людей проклинать?
Чи ти волієш на сцену—з високих котурнів
[віщати,
Чи в героїчних рядках славити війни та кров,

Щоб велемовний учитель виспівував твір твій у
[школі
Й голосом хриплим душив хлопців і чемних дівчат?
Ні! хай про війни гремлять ті поважні та славні
[писаки,
Що до півночі сидять та переводять свічки,—
Ти-ж свої жарти складай та римською сіллю присолюй,
Хай в отих жартах життя вдачу пізнає свою.
Правда, розсудять не раз, що на вбогій ти дудочці
[граєш,—
Але-ж при дудочці тій голосу сурем не чуть".

НЕСТОРА шлях життьовий переміряла ти, о Филено,
    Поки до темрявих хвиль в царство Плутона
                    [зійшла, —
А не зрівнялась проте з прастарою Сибіллою віком:
    Місяців зо три вона довше топтала свій ряст.
В бозі язик спочива, той язик, що його не здолали б
    Ні ярмаркова юрба, ні Серапіса жерці,
Ні журавлині ключі — над Стримоном курличучи
                     [дальнім,
    Ні голосна дітвора — вранці до шкіл ідучи.
Хто-ж тепер зможе, як ти, до землі причаровувать
                     [місяць?
    Хто-ж тепер зможе, як ти, зводництвом славу добуть?
Буде хай пухом земля, не тужавіє ґрунт над тобою,
    Щоби не тяжко було псам одкопати тебе.

MARCÍÑЛ.
Епіграми IX, 60.
Сабінові, посилаючи
вінок з троянд.

ЗВІДКИ-БИ ви не були: чи зростали в роскішнім
[Тибурі,
Чи червоніли як кров в Пестумських ви квітниках,
Чи в Пренестійських садах садовниця вас позрізала,
А чи красою буяв ваш по Кампанії цвіт, —
Скажем: „Троянди оці завітали з мого Номентану“...
Другу Сабіну тоді видасться кращим вінок.

МАРЦІЯЛ.
Епіграми IX, 81.
Авлові.

АВЛЕ, ти знаєш: читач мене хвалить, слухач
[поважає,
Гудять поети лише: неопрацьований вірш!
Я не вважаю на те. Як справляю бенкет, то волію,
Щоб догодити гостям. Що мені смак кухарів?

MARCIAL.
Епіграми X. 23.

ПРИМ Антоній пройшов без турботи свій шлях
[многоденний—
Сімдесят років прожив, восьмий десяток почав.
В роках минулих, у днях пережитих він думою тоне,
I—недалека уже!—Лета йому не страшна;
Тоне в минулому він і пропащого дня не знаходить,
Прикрих не знає годин... в с е б він хотів пригадать.
Праведна, чиста душа існування поширює грані:
Втіху з минулого п'є—вдвоє живе на землі.

ПРИМІТКИ

Шість латинських поетів, зібраних в цій книжечці, обіймають великий протяг часу од перших десятиліть I-го віку перед Хр. — до початків II-го століття по Хр., коло двохсот років приблизно; маємо ми тут перед собою поезію останніх років республіки, страшних часів державної кризи, що привела до нових форм правління, і нарешті поезію Римської імперії в добу Цезарів і Флавіїв. Складаючись в один суцільний образ р и м с ь к о ї поезії, всі ці поети разом з тим репрезентують ріжні фази в житті римського суспільства, ріжні етапи в розвою латинського поетичного стилю.

Найстарший з них — В а л е р і й К а т у л л (84? — 54 перед Хр.) жив і помер ще до початків горожанської війни; обертався він серед римської молодіжі, що живу участь приймала в тогочасній політичній боротьбі, а часом і сам озивався в політичній злобі дня яскравою і сміливою епіграмою на Цезаря та Цезаріянців. В більших поемах наслідував вишуканих і вчених грецьких поетів Александрійської доби, в дрібних поезіях часто й густо був митцем цілком оригінальним. Мова і вірш Катулла ще не мають тієї викінчености й досконалости, що в пізнішого покоління, але коли взяти під увагу багацтво настроїв, безпосередність чуття, повну відсутність всякої реторики, то в цьому розумінні з Катулла безперечно найбільший лірик Риму.

Далі йдуть В е р г і л і й М а р о н (70 — 19 перед Хр.) і Г о р а ц і й Ф л а к к (65 — 8 перед Хр.). Мало чим молодші од Катулла, вони виростали вже серед инших обставин і по духу надзвичайно од нього далекі. Пригрітий новими господарями, дрібний землевласник Ломбардії—Вергілій, син визволеного раба і вигаслий республіканець—Горацій, обидва вірно служать новому режимові: Вергілій, утворюючи династичний і патріотичний епос („Енеїда“);

Горацій, воюючи за нього зброєю своєї сатири і патріотичної оди. Обидва прекрасні стилізатори; обидва додержуються грецьких зразків, майстерно їх на римський ґрунт пересажують. Обидва нарешті незрівняні майстри що до форми: вони до найвищої досконалости доводять поетичний стиль, репрезентуючи собою золотий вік римської поезії.

В особі П р о п е р ц і я (47? — 15 перед Хр.) і О в и д і я Н а з о н а (43 перед Хр. — 17 по Хр.) перед нами знову нова генерація і нова школа літературна. Коли Горацій і Вергілій йшли в свій творчости од Гомера і Сапфо, од грецького епосу і класичної лірики, то покоління Проперція та Овідія звертається до ученої й манєрної поезії Александрійських поетів. Основною літературною формою стає так звана е л е г і я,—це середнього розміру п'єса еротичного змісту, начинена всякою мітологичною вченістю. Елегії звичайно в'яжуться в цікли, присвячені улюбленій дам¹ (часом вигаданій, а часом реальній). Проперцій чистий лірик. Занадто, як на наш погляд, вишуканий і манєрний, він в основі своїй завжди щирий і правдивий; вигаданих ситуацій у нього немає У другого з наведених нами елегіків, у Овидія, літературщина вже переважає: „Елегія Овидія тільки форма, що дісталась йому на спадок од попередніх поетів і первісний зміст уже втратила." Уступаючи Проперцію, як поет кохання, Овидій далеко переважає його як епік („Метаморфози", „Календарь"), а як техник, як майстер віршу стоїть поряд з Горацієм та Вергілієм. Патріотичні мотиви — не чужі Овидієві (почасти й Проперцієві), але його патріотика — невисокого розбору. Коли Вергілій і Горацій, служивши монархії, зберігали певну гідність, Овидій не знає вже міри в своїх славословіях на честь римської могутности і самого Цезаря Августа.

В а л е р і й М а р ц і я л (41? — 104? по Хр.) одділений од Овидія цілим століттям. Він — сучасник імператора Доміціяна, клієнт всесильних його улюбленців. Родом із Іспанії, людина незаможна й залежна, Марціял безбожно курить ладан перед Доміціяном і його камергерами, говорить иноді мовою раба. Немає в нього і твердих моральних принципів. Але зате в нього багато щиросердности, багато дотепу. І вірш його надзвичайно влуч-

ний, стислий, з несподіваними поворотами, пересипаний калам-
бурами, показує в ньому визначного артиста. В історії римської
літератури він має значіння, як творець епіграми в широкому розумінні слова, тоб то невеличкого вірша ліричного змісту, краса
якого вся полягає у влучности стислого виразу.

Розуміється, всі перечислені поети не дають вичерпую-
чого поняття про римську поезію в цілому. В збірнику немає ні
Лукреція, ні Тибулла, ні Ювенала, — а це все імена першорядні —
але перекладчику хтілось би думати, що і в такому вигляді його
книжечка матиме значіння, як один з перших кроків на шляху
засвоєння українським поетичним стилем великого спадку антич-
них літератур.

КАТУЛЛ, 11 (стор. 8).

А в р е л і й і Ф у р і й—К а т у л л о в і д р у з і. Іронія
Аврелій і Фурій—знайомі Катулла; являються до нього з реторич-
ними запевненнями своєї приязні і дипломатичними якимись до-
рученнями від бувшої коханої Катуллової—Клодії (Лесбії). Мож-
ливо, мають на оці помирити її з поетом.

Н а м о р е І н д і й с ь к е і т. д. Непрошені друзі запев-
няють, що готові піти за Катуллом на край світа.—Саки, араби,
парти (парфяне)—народи, суміжні з найдальшими східними провін-
ціями Римської держави. Араби ніжні — molles — звичайний їх
епітет у римських поетів: з Аравії привозились пахучі масла й
смоли.

В д о л и н и, д е Ц е з а р ь... Поезія написана коло 54 р.
перед Хр., коли римське суспільство з великим інтересом стежи-
ло за експедиціями Цезаря за Рейн і в невідому Британію.

КАТУЛЛ, 26 (стор. 10).

Н і А в с т р, н і А п е л ь й о т... Ф а в о н і й і Б о р е й...
Австр (Австер) сухий вітер з півдня, з африканських степів. Нині в Італії його звуть сіроко. Порівняй Горацій, Сатири II, 6.
Апельйот—східний вітер, Борей—північний, Фавоній (Зефір)—за-
хідний.

Н а ш д і м з а с т а в л е н и й з а д в і с т і т и с я ч—
двісті тисяч сестерціїв. Сестерцій—дрібна монета, приблизно 5—6
коп. на срібло. Загальна сума 200 тисяч сестерціїв виносить коло
10—12 тисяч карбованців сріблом.

КАТУЛЛ, 27 (стор. 11).

Давнього Фалерну. Фалерн— одно з найкращих італійських вин. Давнє, видержане, воно було дуже міцне і трохи гіркувате на смак.

Постуміі-цариці. Всі присутні на бенкеті, звичайно, обірали голову учти. На обов'язку такого magister convivii лежала довинність визначити пропорцію вина і води в чашах, з яких присутні черпали вино. Всупереч доброму звичаю, магістра Постумія наказує пити чисте, не розведене водою вино. На вечірках старосвітських, провінціяльних таких звичаів часом не додержувались і особистого смаку гостей не зв'язували. Порівн. Горацій, Сатири II, 6:

П'ємо, та немає ніяких

Правил у нас божевільних і кожний п'е по охоті.

Термін „магістра" перекладаємо словом „цариця", по аналогії з таким виразом, як „цариця балю".. У Пушкина, в його незрівняному перекладі цієі п'єси, читаємо:

Так Постумія веліла

Предсідательница оргій.

КАТУЛЛ, 46 (стор. 12).

Фригіі ниви. Вірш цей написано Катуллом під час його пробування в Малій Азіі. Фригія, Азія—малоазійські провінціі; Никея — головне місто одноі з тих провінцій — Бітиніі.

Український переклад п'єси — Т. Франко. З чужоі левади, Льв. 1913.

ВЕРГІЛІЙ, I ЕКЛОГА (стор. 13).

Написав іі Вергілій коло 41 р. перед Хр., в трівожні дні великоі Італійськоі революціі, в часи упадку старого республікапського Риму і тріумфу нового Цезаріянського з Октавіяном (Августом) на чолі.

Найбільшою опорою переможців були давні легіони Цезаря, що на своїх плечах винесли весь тягарь його гальської та цівільної війни. Тому — задовольнити ветеранів забитого диктатора, надгородити вірних спільників і друзів — стало першим завданням Цезаріянського уряду. Спосіб задоволення був єдиний, підказаний традицією — наділення землею. Але перевести таку величезну операцію земельну тай перевести до того планово й мирно, у правительства жадної змоги не було: земельний фонд Італії був обмежений, ветеранів — багато, скуповувати-ж ґрунта у землевласників за високі ціни — не ставало коштів. Довелось звернутися до методу конфискацій — одібрати землю на території 18 найбагатших міст Італії і заснувати там колонії ветеранів. Налякана розпорядженнями урядових комисарів, тероризована сваволею жовнірства, хліборобська людність Італії доходить до правдивої розпуки: одна частина її шукає виходу в еміграції, друга, зоставшись на місці, ув'язується в криваві сутички з новими власниками, третя—поповнює кадри бандитів та жебраків... Повсякчасні хвилювання й заколоти занепокоїли зрештою й правительство, і Октавіян мусів де в чому свої аграрні закони змягчити: разом з маєтками сенаторів він увільнив од конфискати землі і тих дрібних господарів, що їх власність не перевищувала норми звичайного жовнірського наділу. „Ці льготи, пише Фереро, трохи потішили середні класи, і серед страшного заколоту ніжний та гармонійний голос поета заспівав пісню подяки, якій суджено було лунати на протязі віків. Вергілій, що сам був дрібним землевласником, наважився трактувати в буколічній поезії те, що ми назвали-б нині з л о б о ю д н я. Він висловив в першій еклозі свою подяку і подяку дрібних землевласників Італійських молодому владарю, якого ще й сам гаразд не знав, примішуючи до неї де-що з тієї побожности, яка після апотеозу Цезаря мала тенденцію поширюватися з мертвого фундатора на живих ватажків народньої партії“...

В еклозі проходить перед нами поетичний пейзаж рідної поетові Ломбардії і — на тлі його — розмова двох пастухів, Титира (самого поета) і Мелібея. Мелібей, вигнанний ветераном із свого власного маєтку, дивується товаришові, що зумів серед такої страшної хуртовини оборонити свій хутір та худобу, а той, одповідаючи, починає прославляти молодого Цезаря (Октавіяна), як бога, що подарував йому спокій, вернувши худобу і ґрунт. Він обіцяє приносити на олтарь його найкращих ягнят, клянеться повік йому вірно служити. „Надто вчасний апотеоз на другий день після кривавих проскрипцій!" — зауважає з цього приводу Г. Буасьє, а другий авторитетний дослідник римської старовини докидає: „От коли в літературі римській повіяло новим духом, от де початки римської поезії імператорської доби і остання межа старого республіканського письменства."

Ці слова коротенько, але виразно окреслюють культурноісторичне та історично-літературне значіння еклоги.

Що ж до літературної форми — і д и л і ї, е к л о г и, то вона запозичена Вергілієм у грецького поета III в. перед Хр. — сиціліиця Теокрита. Звідси і заклик поета до „Сицілійських муз" (на початку IV-ої еклоги), і грецькі імена його героїв — Дафніси, Галатеї, Амарілли і т. п., і та згадка про гіблейських бжіл (Гіблою звалось кілька міст в Сицілії), і той гнучкий та мелодійний, на короткі строфи розбитий, окрилений анафорами та алітераціями, гекзаметр.

ВЕРГІЛІЙ, IV ЕКЛОГА (стор. 18).

В багатьох виданнях ця еклога має назву „Полліон" по імени видатного державного діяча часів Августа—Азинія Полліона, котрому присвячена.

В основі еклоги лежить вельми росповсюджений в тодішньому римському громадянстві погляд, ниби-то незабаром має наступити велика світова катастрофа: зорі мають незабаром скластися на ту саму констеляцію, що й на початку світу, і всі пережиті землею епохи мають повторитися наново. Після кривавих горожанських війн кінця республіки — останні тремтіння залізного віку!—настане (і то не в довгім часі) золота доба, щасливий вік Сатурна: знову повернуться на землю боги і між ними Діва-Правда, що останньою полишила колись сплямованих гріхом людей.

Золотий вік змальовано згідно з традицією: земля одпочиває від оранки, на тернових кущах висять важкі китиці винограду, золотий мед виступає на дубовому листі...

Першим владикою нових часів, що по всьому світу „зростить золоте покоління," і буде той дивний хлопчик, якого народження вітає земля і небо. Хто був цей хлопчик, що йому таку світлу долю віщував Вергілій, напевно невідомо. На думку одних дослідників це син Полліона Азиній Галл, на думку других—сподіваний син самого Августа від першої його дружини Скрибонії Не бракує і инших гіпотез (див. проф. О. Зєлинській. Первое свѣтопреставленіе. Изъ жизни идей, т. I.) Христіянські письменники IV-V в. (Лактанцій, бл. Августин) зрозуміли еклогу, як пророцтво про народження Христа. В цьому їх переконали піднесений тон вірша, яскраві картини та урочисті обіцянки, це тремтіння радости, що пробігає по всій природі, а надто символіка, така подібна до символіки святого письма: Змій, що має загинути, згадки про первісний гріх; „потомок богів", посланий на землю..

Середні віки, ідучи за св. батьками, поставили Вергілія в один ряд з старозавітними пророками. Згідно з одною середньовічною легендою, св. Павел, одвідавши у Неаполі могилу поета, окропив її росою святих своїх сліз і сказав: „Когоб я зробив з тебе, як би знайшов живого, найбільший з поетів!" Цігую з Буасьє— La religion Romaine:

Ad Maronis mausoleum
Ductus, fudit super eum
Piae rorem lacrimae:
Quem te, inquit, reddidissem,
Si te vivum invenissem,
Poëtarum maxime!

ГОРАЦІЙ, ОДИ I, 32. ДО ЛІРИ (стор. 25).

На Лесбосі вперше озвався спів твій. Горацій дивиться на себе, як на спадкоємця Лебійських поетів Алкея (600 р. перед Хр.) і Сапфо. Вірш витримано в так званій сапфиній строфі, яка складається з трьох дев'ятискладових — сапфиних рядків і одного п'ятискладового — versus Adonius.

ГОРАЦІЙ, ОДИ I, 38. ДО ХЛОПЦЯ-ПРИСЛУЖНИКА (стор. 26).

Розмір — сапфина строфа.

ГОРАЦІЙ, ОДИ II, 3. ДО ДЕЛЛІЯ (стор. 27).

Вірш цей адресований до Деллія, одного дрібного політичного діяча і публіциста часів Августа. Горацій проповідує йому ясність духа, далекого од трівог і принад буденного життя — aequam mentem, рівновагу філософа. Порівняй українську травестію Гулака-Артемовського „До Пархома":

Пархоме! в щасті не брикай...

ГОРАЦІЙ, ОДИ III, 26. ДО ВЕНЕРИ (стор. 29).

Всякий, хто зрікався привичних занять, посвячував відповідному богові знаряддя своєі роботи. Горацій покидає службу Венері, і складає до ніг народженоі з моря богині непотрібні йому інструменти.

ГОРАЦІЙ, ОДИ IV, 7. ДО ТОРКВАТА (стор. 30).

В темнім житлі, де владика Еней... Мисль поетова така: в темних селищах підземного царства будемо ми всі, без жадних виняткив, навіть царі і герої. (Тулл) Гостилій і Анк (Марцій) — легендарні царі Рима.

Не звільнила свого Іпполіта навіть Діяна сама. Іпполіт—царевич Атен, син Тесея, мисливець і женоненавистник, улюбленець богині Діяни.

Мінос—владика Крита, по смерти—суддя в підземному
царстві.

Піритой, цар лапітів, вірний товариш царя Атенського (Афинського) Тесея. Сміливий і нестримний, „ненавистник богів", цар лапітів намовив Тесея зійти до підземного царства і
викрасти з царського палацу дружину самого Плутона, богиню Прозерпіну. Друзям не повезло, і обидва вони були прикуті до скелі.
Тесея визволив Геракл, вертаючись з Тартара з трьохголовим псом
Цербером, а Піритой так прикутий і зостався, бо в Тесея не
стало сили розірвати на ньому кайдани.

ГОРАЦІЙ, САТИРИ ІІ, 6 (стор.32).

Коло 35 р. перед Хр, ще на початку літературної слави
Горація, Меценат подарував йому невеликий маєток в Сабінських горах, недалеко від Риму. Кількома роками пізніше, восени
31 р. поет написав там найкращу з своїх сатир, присвячену радощам сільського життя.

...і приязнь Геракла здобувши… В Італії
Геракла шановано, як бога-виказчика прихованих скарбів.

**Щоб худоба моя (аби тільки не розум!)
сита була...** Ситий, налитий салом розум (pingue ingenium)—
означення тупої, обмеженої людини.

Та тільки зійду я на Есквилин... Горацій,
вставши з ліжка, біжить спочатку ручитись за свого приятеля на
форум, а звідти на Есквилинську гору, де жив Меценат. Це ранішній, обов'язковий для кожного клієнта візит.

Скріби на збори тебе закликають. Горацій один час займав посаду в квесторській канцелярії. Хтось з
його товаришів, зустрівшись з ним в Меценатовій господі, нагадує йому про засідання в якійсь спільній справі (de re communi)

Запрошати до власної реди. Реда (Raeda,
rheda) легка коляска.

Що там чувати про даків. Даки в нинішнім Семигороді та Румунії. В 31 році перед Хр. боялись їхнього походу в північну Італію.

...родичів Пітагора—боби я побачу. Пітагор (математик, філософ, релігійний реформатор) забороняв своїм учням їсти боби. Вигадано було й пояснення,—ніби-то він твердив, що люде й боби одного походження.

Я й мої гості їмо перед ларом. Вечеря одбувається, згідно з старовинним звичаєм, перед ларами(статуями родових богів)—тоб-то в великій світлиці, в атрії, а не в спеціально оборудованій ідальні, трикліні́ї.

Ареллій — невідомий ближче негоціянт, що мав, очевидно, немало клопоту через своє багацтво.

Ніби той раб підперезаний. Сільське мишеня, хоч і вбоге, але приймає свого гостя з почуттям власної гідности, по хазяйски; міське, в багатому домі, поводиться, як проворний і пронирливий раб в підперезаній (в інтересах більшої слободи рухів) туніці. Цікава паралель сільського господаря і міського паразита.

ПРОПЕРЦІЙ, ЕЛЕГІЇ III, 2 (стор. 38).

Скелі з гірських верховин... Відома легенда про будування міської стіни в Тебах. Царь Тебанський, Амфіон. збудував її, користаючись виключно своїм музичним хистом. Цей самий мотив знаходимо у Лесі Українки, в її драматичній поемі „Орфеєве чудо" (Ювилейний збірник, присвячений Франкові, в 40-ліття його діяльности).

Навіть на голос твоїх, Поліфеме, пісень... Поліфем—ціклоп, Галатея—нимфа. Закоханий Поліфем—сюжет одної з ідилій самого законодавця ідилії — Теокрита, грецького поета III віку перед Хр.

Сад мій не рівня гаям феакійським... На острові феаків, що привітали Одиссея на путі до рідного краю. був величезний сад. Його опис в 7-ій пісні Гомерової „Одиссеї":

Сад превеликий за двором од самих воріт починавси,

Він навкруги парканом обгорожений був; по тім саду

Різна росла деревина, зелена та рясна й пахуча:
Яблуні, груші, гранати, одно од другого смашніші,
Смокви з солодшим од меду плодом і товстії маслини.
Овочі родять на них цілий рік — і зімою, і літом.
Западовець, що там віє раз-в-раз, їх зрощає по черзі;
Инше то тільки ростить ще, а инше то вже наливає.

(Перекл. П. Ніщинського).

К а л л і о п а — одна з дев'яти муз.

Н а м о г и л ь н о г о д о м у М а в з о л а. Надгробок Ка-
рійського царя Мавзола (мавзолей) уважали одним з 7 див все-
світніх.

ОВИДІЙ, НА СМЕРТЬ ТИБУЛЛА (стор. 40).

Альбій Тибулл (54 — 19 перед Хр.) найстарший з римських елегиків (майстрів любовної лірики), твори яких дійшли до
нас; наймолодший—Овидій; середнє місце належить Проперцію.

М а т и А х и л л а й М е м н о н а. Ахилла — син богині
Тетиди; Мемнон — син Аврори (Зорі).

С и н А ф р о д и т и — Ерот (Амур).

Я к б р а т а Е н е я х о в а л и. Еней — так само син Венери (Афродити); отже Еротові він доводиться братом. Іюл — син
Енея.

Л ю б и й ю н а к, в е п р о м п о р а в е н и й... Пастух Адо-
нис, улюбленець Венери.

В н е т р я х з а г и н у в і Л і н. Лін — легендарний співець, друг Орфея, що перейняв поетичний дар од самих богів.
Пор. Вергілієву IV еклогу.

М е о н и д — Гомер.

П і є р и д и — Музи

В ч о р н і м А в е р н і... Аверн — багниста місцевість в
середній Італії, недалечко од Кум, де жила знаменита Сибілла, в
Кампанській рівнині. Авернське озеро уважали входом до підземного царства.

Д е л і я і Н е м е з и с а — героіні любовних елегій Тибулла.

є г и п е т с ь к и х с и с т р і в. Систр — музичний інстру-
мент єгипетського походження, брязкало.

МАРЦІЯЛ, ЕПІГРАМИ VIII, 3 (стор. 42).

Н а д г р о б о к М е с с а л и. Валерій Мессала — держав-
ний діяч і літературний патрон часів Августа.

М а р м у р Л і ц і н а. Ліцін, визволений раб імператора
Августа, був якийсь час намістником Галлії. На протязі свого
управління провінцією, набув собі неправедні, але великі маєтки.
Пізніше всі скарби його було сконфисковано; де-що проте йому
вдалось урятувати. На ті рештки колишнього багацтва він нака-
зав поставити собі розкішний пам'ятник, що нарівні з мавзолеєм
Мессали увійшов в оборот щоденної розмови.

Д е в ' я т а з с е с т е р. Одна з дев'яти Муз.

МАРЦІЯЛ, ЕПІГРАМИ ІХ, 29 (стор. 44).

Н е с т о р а ш л я х ж и т т ь о в и й. Нестор — найстарі-
ший з героїв Гомерівських поем, що пережив три покоління
людські.

МАРЦІЯЛ, ЕПІГРАМИ ІХ, 60 (стор. 45).

...в Т и б у р і р о с к і ш н і м з р о с т а л и. Тибур, Пре-
неста, Пестум — італійські міста, славетні своїми квітниками.

...з м о г о Н о м е н т а н у. Номентан — місто в Середній Італії, в околиці якого була невелика віла Марціялова.

───────

ЗМІСТ.

Contributors

Olga Bertelsen is an Associate Professor of Global Security and Intelligence at Tiffin University's School of Criminal Justice and Social Science/Homeland Security & Terrorism. Educated at the Medical State University, Ukraine, Bloomsburg University of Pennsylvania, U.S., Penn State University, U.S., and the University of Nottingham, U.K., she published widely on Soviet/Russian active measures, operations of ideological subversion, the strategies and tactics of the Soviet secret police, and state and political violence, and edited anthologies of archival documents on Les Kurbas and persecutions of Jews in Ukraine. She is the editor of *Revolution and War in Contemporary Ukraine and Russian Active Measures*, and the author of *The House of Writers in Ukraine, the 1930s*, and *In the Labyrinth of the KGB*.

Polly Corrigan became an intern at *The Guardian* in 1996 and a writer with the dotcom company *Wide Learning* in 1998. In 2003 she joined *Telegraph Online*, becoming its first features editor, and early on inadvertently posting an entire Jeffrey Archer novel before publication, an error that earned only the briefest of reprimands.

She stayed in the job for six years, but then her life changed direction with the birth of her children, Martha (in 2006) and Rosie (in 2009). In 2009, she gave up full-time work to devote herself to their care.

Three years ago, she embarked on a doctoral thesis at KCL department of war studies. The subject, the systems behind the Great Terror in the USSR in the 1930s, gave her a leading role within an international group of academics reconsidering how a regime promising utopian-style freedom instead delivered terror and tyranny. She contributed a chapter, *Walking the Razor's Edge: The Origins of Soviet Censorship*, to the Bloomsbury publication, *The Fate of the Bolshevik Revolution, Illiberal Liberation, 1917-1941*, published in 2020.

Victoria A. Malko is a faculty member and founding coordinator of the Holodomor Studies Program in the Department of History at California State University, Fresno. She is the author of *The Chechen*

Wars: Responses in Russia and the United States (2015) *and editor of Women and the Holodomor-Genocide: Victims, Survivors, Perpetrators* (2019). She is the author of "Russian (Dis)Information Warfare vis-a-vis the Holodomor-Genocide" in a collective monograph *Russian Active Measures: Yesterday, Today, Tomorrow*, edited by Olga Bertelsen (2021). Her new monograph *The Ukrainian Intelligentsia and Genocide: The Struggle for History, Language, and Culture in the 1920s and 1930s* was published in 2021 by Lexington Books, an imprint of Rowman & Littlefield. She serves on the editorial board of *American History and Politics*.

Joe Wallmannsberger is professor of computational linguistics at the University of Kassel, Germany. As a native Austrian he was educated in Classics, Linguistics and Philosophy at the universities of Innsbruck, Salzburg, Konstanz and Stanford. After academic appointments the universities of Leicester, Innsbruck and Siegen, he assumed his current role at Kassel University. He was inducted to the highly arcane order of aficionados of Ukrainian neoclassicist literature during conversations with Polish and Ukrainian scholars in the basement cafeteria at Humboldt University, East Berlin: both the city and the scholar have fittingly opted to continue their existence in parallel imaginaries ever open for semiotic walkabouts.

Mykola Zerov figures among the immortals of the Ukrainian poetic, literary and artistic tradition. His 'professor hat' worn during his stay at the Solovki political prisoner camp serves as a constant and painful reminder of what professor heads are supposed to cover, admittedly in an academic sanctuary of future philologists.

UKRAINIAN VOICES

Collected by Andreas Umland

Sergiy Korsunsky, Kobe Gakuin University, Japan

Nadiia Koval, Kyiv School of Economics, Ukraine

Volodymyr Kravchenko, University of Alberta, Edmonton

Oleksiy Kresin, NAS Koretskiy Institute of State and Law, Kyiv

Anatoliy Kruglashov, Fedkovych National University, Chernivtsi

Andrey Kurkov, PEN Ukraine, Kyiv

Ostap Kushnir, Lazarski University, Warsaw

Taras Kuzio, National University of Kyiv-Mohyla Academy

Serhii Kvit, National University of Kyiv-Mohyla Academy

Yuliya Ladygina, The Pennsylvania State University, USA

Yevhen Mahda, Institute of World Policy, Kyiv

Victoria Malko, California State University, Fresno, USA

Yulia Marushevska, Security and Defense Center (SAND), Kyiv

Myroslav Marynovych, Ukrainian Catholic University, Lviv

Oleksandra Matviichuk, Center for Civil Liberties, Kyiv

Mykhailo Minakov, Kennan Institute, Washington, USA

Anton Moiseienko, The Australian National University, Canberra

Alexander Motyl, Rutgers University-Newark, USA

Vlad Mykhnenko, University of Oxford, United Kingdom

Vitalii Ogiienko, Ukrainian Institute of National Remembrance, Kyiv

Olga Onuch, University of Manchester, United Kingdom

Olesya Ostrovska, Museum "Mystetskyi Arsenal," Kyiv

Anna Osypchuk, National University of Kyiv-Mohyla Academy

Oleksandr Pankieiev, University of Alberta, Edmonton

Oleksiy Panych, Publishing House "Dukh i Litera," Kyiv

Valerii Pekar, Kyiv-Mohyla Business School, Ukraine

Yohanan Petrovsky-Shtern, Northwestern University, Chicago

Serhii Plokhy, Harvard University, Cambridge, USA

Andrii Portnov, Viadrina University, Frankfurt-Oder, Germany

Maryna Rabinovych, Kyiv School of Economics, Ukraine

Valentyna Romanova, Institute of Developing Economies, Tokyo

Natalya Ryabinska, Collegium Civitas, Warsaw, Poland

Darya Tsymbalyk, University of Oxford, United Kingdom

Vsevolod Samokhvalov, University of Liege, Belgium

Orest Semotiuk, Franko National University, Lviv

Viktoriya Sereda, NAS Institute of Ethnology, Lviv

Anton Shekhovtsov, University of Vienna, Austria

Andriy Shevchenko, Media Center Ukraine, Kyiv

Oxana Shevel, Tufts University, Medford, USA

Pavlo Shopin, National Pedagogical Dragomanov University, Kyiv

Karina Shyrokykh, Stockholm University, Sweden

Nadja Simon, freelance interpreter, Cologne, Germany

Olena Snigova, NAS Institute for Economics and Forecasting, Kyiv

Ilona Solohub, Analytical Platform "VoxUkraine," Kyiv

Iryna Solonenko, LibMod - Center for Liberal Modernity, Berlin

Galyna Solovei, National University of Kyiv-Mohyla Academy

Sergiy Stelmakh, NAS Institute of World History, Kyiv

Olena Stiazhkina, NAS Institute of the History of Ukraine, Kyiv

Dmitri Stratievski, Osteuropa Zentrum (OEZB), Berlin

Dmytro Stus, National Taras Shevchenko Museum, Kyiv

Frank Sysyn, University of Toronto, Canada

Olha Tokariuk, Center for European Policy Analysis, Washington

Olena Tregub, Independent Anti-Corruption Commission, Kyiv

Hlib Vyshlinsky, Centre for Economic Strategy, Kyiv

Mychailo Wynnyckyj, National University of Kyiv-Mohyla Academy

Yelyzaveta Yasko, NGO "Yellow Blue Strategy," Kyiv

Serhy Yekelchyk, University of Victoria, Canada

Victor Yushchenko, President of Ukraine 2005-2010, Kyiv

Oleksandr Zaitsev, Ukrainian Catholic University, Lviv

Kateryna Zarembo, National University of Kyiv-Mohyla Academy

Yaroslav Zhalilo, National Institute for Strategic Studies, Kyiv

Sergei Zhuk, Ball State University at Muncie, USA

Alina Zubkovych, Nordic Ukraine Forum, Stockholm

Liudmyla Zubrytska, National University of Kyiv-Mohyla Academy